People, Poverty and Shelter

People, Poverty and Shelter

PROBLEMS OF SELF-HELP HOUSING IN THE THIRD WORLD

Edited by
R. J. SKINNER and M. J. RODELL

METHUEN
LONDON AND NEW YORK

First published in 1983 by
Methuen & Co. Ltd
11 New Fetter Lane, London EC4P 4EE
Published in the USA by
Methuen & Co.
in association with Methuen, Inc.
733 Third Avenue, New York, NY 10017

Typeset by Scarborough Typesetting Services
and printed in Great Britain at the
University Press, Cambridge

British Library Cataloguing in Publication Data

People, poverty and shelter.
1. Self-help housing – Underdeveloped areas
I. Skinner, R. J.   II. Rodell, M. J.
363.5'8   HD7287.5
ISBN 0-416-30960-7

Library of Congress Cataloging in Publication Data

Main entry under title:
People, poverty, and shelter.
Includes index.
1. Underdeveloped areas—Self-help housing.
I. Skinner, R. J.   II. Rodell, M. J. (Michael J.)
(Reinhard J.), 1950–
HD7391.P46   1983   363.5'8'091724   83-7967
ISBN 0-416-30960-7 (U.S.: pbk.)

Contents

List of illustrations

List of tables

List of contributors

PAUL BAROSS, a planner with the Institute for Housing Studies in Rotterdam since 1974, was project leader for the Institute in establishing, with the Indonesian government, a joint housing, planning and design training centre in Bandung between 1978 and 1981. Since 1970 he has also researched, or acted as consultant, in various countries including Canada, Burma, Papua New Guinea and Thailand.

PATRICK CROOKE is an architect-planner who has been involved in research, consultancy, teaching and practitioner capacities in a variety of organizations related to low-income housing in the Third World. He has worked for the ILO, the United Nations Centre for Housing, Building and Planning, the University of Khartoum, the Ministry of Public Education in Peru and the Universidad de los Andes in Bogotá, Colombia. In addition, his private consultancy work has taken him to urban and rural housing projects in Indonesia, Malaysia, Egypt and Malawi, apart from postgraduate teaching in Britain, Colombia, Tanzania and Thailand.

INGO GUHR is an architect currently working in a multidisciplinary team renovating the ancient buildings of Bhaktapur, Nepal. Prior to this he had been a UN senior expert attached to the Ministry of Lands, Housing and Urban Development in Tanzania where he developed a special concern for co-operative housing. Other work has taken him to West Germany, Thailand and Malawi in teaching, consultative, research and practitioner roles, including two years at the Institute for Housing Studies, Rotterdam.

RICHARD MARTIN is a planner currently employed by USAID in Kenya. Before that he had been a staff member of the Institute for

Housing Studies, Rotterdam which involved him in teaching in training centres in Thailand and Tanzania. Until 1979 he had worked for eleven years in Zambia, mainly on low-cost or self-help housing for the National Housing Authority and was Deputy Director of the Lusaka squatter upgrading and sites and services programme.

MICHAEL RODELL, a planner, has worked at the Institute for Housing Studies in Rotterdam since 1975. There he teaches housing finance in addition to having developed, and taught, courses in Tanzania and Thailand. He previously lectured in economics at the Federal University of Bahia in Brazil.

REINHARD SKINNER is a sociologist who co-ordinates a workshop on state and community in low-income housing development at the Institute for Housing Studies, Rotterdam, where he has been since 1977. He has appraised training projects for housing professionals in Colombia, Ecuador and Peru, and has lectured in training centres in Tanzania, Thailand, Colombia and Sri Lanka.

EMIEL WEGELIN is an economist who, before moving to the Asian Development Bank in 1982, had worked at the Centre for Housing and Human Settlements Studies, National Housing Authority of Thailand, as project leader of a joint Dutch-Thai technical co-operation venture. Previously, he had evaluated low-cost housing projects in Malaysia and worked in the planning and implementation of slum improvement projects in Pakistan.

Acknowledgements

No book ever gets to the press by the efforts of the authors alone. Here the editors can at least give some small recognition to the considerable assistance afforded them by those who have suffered and encouraged in the production of this volume. Yvonne Barendrecht, Anneke Mohr, Hannie Plomp and Hanny van den Bosch all somehow managed to escape an already heavy workload at the Institute for Housing Studies to type the book at its various stages. Tiersa Rodell also allowed herself to become ensnared in this endeavour, while Geraldine Skinner insisted that the proof-reading was done and corrections made.

1
Introduction: contemporary self-help programmes

M. J. RODELL and R. J. SKINNER

1.1 Self-help programmes

The implementation of housing policy is very much an experimental activity from formulation to final forms. Policies start somewhere in discussions about housing problems, how they come about, and, given an experience with attempted solutions, what seems to work or not work in practice. During the 1950s and 1960s, the nearly universal formula for housing policy held that the enormous growth of slum and squatter housing stemmed from people's inability to pay for conventional housing and furthermore government would solve the problem by building and subsidizing the necessary units. The experience of this attempted solution, especially the failure of even well-funded programmes to house many people, suggested that governments would not or could not mobilize enough resources to make it work. The resulting absence of public housing leaves families no choices beyond renting in slums or building houses on their own, as and when they can.

Today the old formula has been replaced by a new framework of ideas about housing policy. It starts from the observation that families do indeed build a large part of the low-income housing stock. Where their results fall short of desired standards, poverty is not always the cause. Indeed many people slowly manage to build substantial dwellings, but are hampered in their efforts by the risk of being relocated and the lack of adequate sites, public services, and construction credit. The new policy formula now asks government to supply the missing elements and, in effect, to incorporate self-help into public housing programmes. By combining the housing investments of families and government, governments might reduce their investment per family and so reach a larger number of families, thus helping to overcome the main deficiency − low access − which resulted from conventional housing policy.

The self-help framework lends itself to far more variation in practice than one is likely to find among conventional programmes. There is a long succession of self-help projects, pilot schemes, organized by volunteer groups and charities throughout the Third World. Some of the socialist countries have had large programmes for organizing factory and farm workers in producing their own houses. The models for these efforts trace back to Europe in the nineteenth century, and even then were a focus of controversy (Engels 1975). In this tradition a housing agency organizes residents to do a large part of the work in what are otherwise conventional housing projects. Contemporary self-help programmes, in contrast, differ widely in what they attempt to produce and how they go about this. At one extreme, an agency merely upgrades an old squatter neighbourhood by removing the threat of eviction and adding some infrastructure. House improvements are still left entirely in the hands of families. At the other extreme, an agency develops new neighbourhoods with incomplete houses and construction loans for extensions and improvements of houses. In between lies an almost infinite number of possible combinations between governmental and family investment in housing.

1.2 Policy issues

Undeniably housing agencies in the Third World do not have the funds to house all poor families at the standards adopted in the 1950s and 1960s. Countries, broadly, fall into three categories. One group has not the resources for conventional standards. A second perhaps has the resources, but governments in this group either have left control over the economy in private hands or have devoted only a tiny share of public resources to housing. A third group falls in between and is constituted by countries whose governments could dramatically increase public spending on housing, but not enough to house everyone. In all three groups, conventional housing failed to reach many low-income families, and this has been used to justify changing over to the forms of self-help embodied in upgrading and sites and services.

Upgrading and sites and services might improve the chances for poor families to benefit from governmental housing investment in three ways, besides self-help. Immediately, the money government would need to house one family conventionally can provide several with serviced plots or with basic infrastructure in old neighbourhoods. The physical consequences of this − incomplete housing and new services added to housing built over a long period of time – have led to these projects being labelled 'evolutionary', 'progressive' or 'gradual construction' housing projects, which signifies not only construction over a long period but, more important, that housing is occupied before it is complete. Some element of gradual construction occurs in all contemporary self-help programmes. This element, rather than self-help, accounts for the pro-grammes' ability to provide access for thousands of families where conventional housing could reach only hundreds.

A second, if less universal element, is relatively low subsidy rates. The rate of subsidy itself governs the amount of revenue an agency collects for repaying debts or reinvesting, and this limits how much investment an agency can finance during a five- or ten-year period. The higher the rate of subsidy, the less investment can be planned. In principle, not all components of a given standard of housing have to be subsidized at the same rate to be affordable. The necessary subsidy on complete housing is in effect an average of, say, low rates for infrastructure and high rates for finished houses.

Hence, initially concentrating on components that require relatively low rates should, over time, increase funds for housing. If they compared conventional to self-help programmes, governments might see that if they spend more money in the latter, the effects reach a correspondingly larger number of families.

The third way of increasing access, of course, is by cutting standards and costs. A great deal of confusion surrounds this issue and its relation to self-help, gradual construction and subsidy rates. When an agency accustomed to providing four-room houses with full services on 200 m^2 plots switches to sites and services projects with no houses, a materials loan for a two-room core, and no individual service connections on 100 m^2, it has reduced standards in its projects. This does not necessarily mean reducing housing standards in a city, for overall standards reflect also the conditions people endure in slums and squatter neighbour-hoods. Possibly, by increasing access, cutting standards in projects can bring enough people out of slums to appreciably raise standards overall.

Moreover, reduced standards are often confused with gradual con-struction, though they are two separate things. A reduction of plot sizes from 200 m^2 to 100 m^2 lowers standards. But leaving individual water connections to be installed some time after families move into a project lowers service standards initially. Nothing prevents service standards reaching the same high level in both conventional and sites and services neighbourhoods. A similar distinction between reduced standards and initially incomplete housing applies to all components that, unlike plot sizes, do not have to be fixed forever to provide someone a place to live.

Gradual construction, relatively low subsidy rates, and reduced standards in projects are then three features of contemporary housing programmes. Though all three are distinct from self-help, decisions about each have profound effects on how self-help works. And, as we shall see in a moment, what governments expect from self-help also influences decisions about gradual construction, subsidy rates, and standards. The relations among these four elements of policy and access constitute the main sources of problems in – and heated controversies over – planning and implementing self-help housing programmes in the Third World.

However, self-help programmes have also raised broader questions about fairness and implications of housing policy for social development. Whereas the majority of conventional public housing consisted of state-owned and allocated units, most self-help housing programmes are installing infrastructure for privately owned houses, giving ownership or long-term transferable leasehold rights, and selling newly developed land. Self-help housing thus becomes part of the formal market, which strengthens liberal forms of development that housing policies used to try to counter and abandons a measure of public control over the distribution of benefits. Burgess (1982), for example, has argued that governments adopt self-help to avoid redistributional and structural changes needed to house people decently. Self-help policies ask people to work long hours, either in construction or to earn money to pay for construction, and thus to take the burden of housing on their own shoulders. To the extent this will ameliorate the worst housing conditions, it reduces pressures for higher and more progressive taxation or for reduced public spending in programmes that benefit mostly middle- and upper-income classes and special interest groups. In this view, self-help programmes reinforce inequities that lie at the root of low-income families' poverty and consequent housing problems.

1.3 The nature of self-help

The concept of self-help underwent a marked transition between the mid-1960s and mid-1970s, roughly dating from the publication of Charles Abrams's *Man's Struggle for Shelter in an Urbanizing World*, in 1964, and John Turner's *Housing by People*, in 1976. Before Abrams's book, self-help was understood in a technological sense. Self-help housing meant houses low-income families constructed with their own, unpaid labour. Abrams (1964: 164, 169) pointed out that this type of housing accounted for most of the houses in the world, today and historically. It was, however, a predominantly rural phenomenon. In an idealized model, families in villages organized the whole production process without paid labour. They plotted land, collected materials, fabricated building components, prepared the site, and assembled the components into a house. The model served as a rough description of what happens in many parts of the world, though in some regions, West Africa for example, even rural housing had old traditions of construction by professional contractors.

As long as cities were small and grew slowly, similar construction occurred in old villages incorporated into the urban fabric and in the native compounds of colonial centres, where municipal authorities ceded land to native classes or accepted traditional landholding systems. Abrams (1964: 165, 173f.) insisted self-help, in the technological sense of houses built by residents' own hands, should be seen as part of a form of life that disappears irretrievably in large, contemporary cities. With this loss (1964: 165), 'Disposal of wastes becomes an almost insuperable health problem. . . . The long trek to and from the job and dependence on the market for land and materials and on community organization for vital services' make self-help unworkable.

This conclusion, of course, had been a major premise of post-World War II housing policy, which gave governmental agencies responsibility for building urban low-income housing. By the time Abrams wrote, these agencies had already failed to expand housing supply sufficiently, and families without any housing and unable to use traditional self-help crowded into slums and started building for themselves in squatter neighbourhoods. During the 1950s, squatter housing shared a single, technological attribute in common with traditional self-help housing: families in both used largely their own unpaid labour to collect materials and assemble houses. In every other way, however, squatter housing was a distinct area, in which choice of land, design of houses, the availability of labour and materials, and societal sanction worked themselves out through conflictive, complicated processes not at all like the traditional self-help systems. The first results inevitably turned out to be either shacks in permanent settlements without any public services, or shanties on sites (e.g. railroad rights of way) families would occupy as long as they had no better alternative and were not forced to move.

Despite these differences between traditional self-help and squatter housing, outsiders, from housing ministers to social anthropologists, attached the 'self-help' label to urban squatter housing, and the label came to mean unpaid family labour. Everyone outside squatter housing tended to think that where families built their own housing, their principal input into house construction was this labour. The idea provided a plausible rationale of the physical attributes that anyone could see in squatter housing. In a city, family labour could not possibly produce appropriate materials, so family labour could only collect the waste materials urban economies generated in abundance. Similarly, family labour in cities was occupied six or seven days a week, fifty-two weeks a year, in earning money and fulfilling daily domestic needs. There was no time between harvests, when a food reserve freed time for intense, community-organized house construction. Each urban house produced by family labour was a quick-built house erected on weekends and at nights. Families organized most construction individually, since they all needed housing at the same time and could not rely on well-housed neighbours to help this year's new families add a few units to the neighbourhood. Finally, the rural migrants who were building squatter housing in the 1950s brought rural skills, which naturally they had to apply in any construction in which they used their own labour.

By the time a city had 100,000 squatter houses and the squatter housing stock was increasing 10–15 per cent a year – two to three times the annual rate of the conventional stock – the identification of self-help with unpaid family labour raised an inescapable question. Suppose each squatter family could invest 1000 hours of unpaid labour; then the squatter stock represents 100 million hours of family labour, increasing each year by the addition of another 10–15 million hours. Could this resource not be used more productively outside squatter housing? Seen from the standpoint of a housing agency, family labour constituted a potentially free addition to the resources governments could incorporate in housing. This view allied itself with the much older idea that family labour reduces unit costs of construction. The marriage of the two notions – an added resource in the production of public housing and a reduction of unit costs – resulted in what Abrams (1964: 168ff.) called the self-help formula:

> Neolithic techniques were 'updated' to include tutorial instruction, and the most modern cost-accounting methods kept track of hours spent and materials used. Speed of block production was increased in pilot areas by more modern hand tools to achieve self-help mass production. Sometimes the program was marked by a missionary element (i.e., 'God helps all those who help themselves'), which became partly responsible for the faith and zeal associated with the expensive programs.

Government provides all the inputs except part of the labour needed to assemble components in a house. Families, aided by professional supervisors, invest the necessary labour. Unpaid family labour in this formula can replace wage labour amounting to between 15 and 30 per cent of the costs of a conventionally constructed project, depending largely on project-to-project variations of land costs and wage rates relative to materials prices. The substitution adds, however, extra costs of tutorial instruction, supervision, and interest, resulting in a net reduction of government's part of a project's costs of between 10 and 20 per cent compared to costs of similar housing built conventionally (Abrams 1964: 174; Angel *et al.* 1981: 11–23).

Within this limit, agencies may design a project, for instance to use family labour only for site preparation and finishings, in which case maximum wage savings may be 3–4 per cent of total costs. Alternatively, a project can employ family labour in the fabrication of building components as well as preparatory and assembly work, reaching the upper limits of wage savings. Transferring wage labour saved this way into infrastructure construction or materials production could then be expected to enable a housing agency to increase its annual production of houses by somewhere between 5 and 20 per cent.

From individual families' point of view, an agency's wage savings translate into correspondingly lower cash payments to offset the personal costs of unpaid labour. There is no precise way fully to compare the cash savings with the costs of family labour. In the case of maximum savings, a family would pay around 20 per cent less money but have to work an additional 1500 to 2000 hours over a year or so. Whether the lower payment improves affordability in terms of a household's budget more than the large labour cost reduces affordability in terms of time available is a question that can be answered only at the family level. The answer will vary from one family to the next. But the magnitudes involved, when payments for a conventional unit would total two-and-a-half times a family's income and the unpaid labour approaches one man-year, suggest that the self-help formula improves affordability in the broad sense only marginally, and only for certain families with abundant time free of work or the search for work during the year or more required for construction.

In a series of reports prepared between 1955 and 1963, Abrams and Otto Koenigsberger formulated the broad outlines of what was to become, by 1975, the most widely accepted framework of urban low-income housing policy. Their 'land-and-utilities schemes' were soon known as (open plot) sites and services. 'Where the aim is not primarily the training of workers,' Abrams wrote (1964: 174), 'it is preferable [instead of aided self-help housing] for the government to lay out and provide plots and utilities and let each owner decide whether to use his own skills or hire others for all, most, or part of the work'. Where government provides more than land and utilities, the Abrams–Koenigsberger proposals advised roof loans, core houses, or small construction loans in place of any attempt to finance complete houses.

The distinctions between this and either traditional or aided self-help housing was, first, a difference between complete and incomplete housing at the time families move into a neighbourhood. In a land and utilities or a core house scheme, houses would be built by instalment construction (Abrams 1964: 175). Acquisition of materials and savings to pay wage labour come in increments. Implicit in this view was a largely individual, slow, irregular process of accumulation.

Second, in the Abrams–Koenigsberger formulations, families decided individually about house designs, materials, labour, and the scheduling of their own investment. Abrams (1964: 173) cites with approval 'so-called self-help projects in Bogota' where the 'house is designed by the owner himself, though the [agency] provides six optional plans'. Technical assistance, rather than as a system for organizing the use of unpaid labour within a pre-defined construction schedule, is designed as a set of services from which each family can select the ones it wants. Both the overall planning of a house and a neighbourhood, which had been a corporate function of a village in traditional self-help and of a housing agency in aided self-help, disappears in the incomplete housing projects Abrams was proposing.

By 1970, of course, sites and services had absorbed both the open plot and core housing proposals under one heading, and this was the pre-eminent point of reference of what self-help housing should be. Abrams's insistence on sites and services as an alternative to self-help could be treated as just a semantic foible, except the issues he raised have still not been resolved in contemporary self-help housing policies.

Abrams had rather modest expectations of sites and services (and by implication of upgrading, which he did not discuss in detail). It achieved its aims by a substantial reduction of unit costs and minimum standards relative to those in conventional and aided self-help projects. He was not advocating a shifting of the burden of high-standard housing to poor families, or compulsory production of the houses governments did not subsidize. It was not self-help in the sense of governmentally organized labour, so it would not produce the same type of standard housing. Some people, Abrams thought, may call the results a slum (1964: 181), but it is an 'alterable and improvable slum. Planned as minimum housing, it will lend itself to adjustment and improvement more than the compromises that obsolesce quickly and leave their sad remains for a century or more.'

Abrams was measuring success in terms of access, and he saw access as a function of (a) government providing whatever could be produced quickly in huge numbers, which will vary from country to country and, within a country, from decade to decade, and (b) families providing costs, what they could afford on top of this. Each family decides a large part of its housing, so that families are not excluded because they cannot afford the expenses or the necessary labour of unsubsidized portions of costs. This solution

> is more a universal recipe for housing shortage than is self-help. . . . It is no substitute for traditional self-help or mutual-aid techniques in the rural area. . . . Often it is more efficient than organized self-help operations now [around 1960] being laboriously launched in cities. (1964: 181)

Abrams had in mind, when he wrote this, laborious aided self-help projects, but his comments are equally applicable to what was then the popular image of squatter housing in which unpaid family labour was the only significant input besides land.

During the 1960s, however, John Turner's studies of squatter housing effectively changed its popular image. Turner's studies had an advantage of ten to twenty years over the studies of squatting in the 1950s. The neighbourhoods which outsiders visited in the early 1950s had just started. Most were precariously built by people, often recent migrants, who believed governments would some day carry out plans for clearance and relocation. When Turner visited them in the late 1960s he found quite different housing. Alongside shacks and shanties, squatter neighbourhoods also had virtually 'standard' houses. Turner found squatter neighbourhoods that could not be visually distinguished from legal, conventionally built housing. Over a decade they had developed from shack to standard houses. In the process Turner described how neighbourhoods developed incrementally or gradually. This was Abrams's 'instalment construction', except that Turner stressed the irregularity of increments, which did not come in the periodic lumps suggested by the term 'instalment'. What Turner termed 'housing by people' characterized the process. In other words, when residents decide about investment, their own aims, their individual circumstances (e.g. incomes over a decade, family characteristics, skills, sources of income), and their group circumstances (e.g. relation with government, community organization) it results in a variety of housing. The designs, materials, proportions of family and wage labour alter over time in relation to varying aims and circumstances. Shacks at the start are self-help, in the pre-1960 sense of the term; they may or may not last a long time. But they are not the sum total of housing by people any more than unpaid labour is the main ingredient of self-help in squatter neighbourhoods. What Turner did was effectively to

Table 1.1 Concepts of urban self-help housing.

Before Abrams (the 1950s)	After Turner (the 1970s)
Basic idea Self-help = unpaid family labour.	*Basic ideas* Self-help = families deciding about investments. Self-help = investment inputs supplied by families, either inputs purchased with cash savings, or unpaid labour, or both.
Examples Shacks and shanties in squatter neighbourhoods.	*Examples* Covers the range from shacks and shanties to standard neighbourhoods.
Construction process 1 Squatted land. 2 Scrap and waste materials. 3 Unpaid labour on weekends and at nights. 4 Construction starts from occupancy, and ends a day to a year after this date. The end-product is constrained by families' incomes during one year, materials costs and illegality of tenure.	*Construction process* 1 Various and unpredictable. Construction can last one day to five, ten or fifteen years. 2 Shacks and shanties can be a final product or an intermediate stage within the process. The end-product is constrained by families' incomes over a decade or more, materials costs and perceived security of tenure
Who uses self-help? Recent migrants from distressed rural areas.	*Who uses self-help?* Anyone can; usually, families who start with self-help are low- to middle-income at the date they start.
Policy implications 1 The basic theory: self-help reduces construction costs of a given type of housing.	*Policy implications* 1 The basic theory: under certain conditions, self-help increases investment in housing because (a) it adds unpaid labour to the resources used in housing; (b) it adds inputs purchased by families to resources used in housing.

Table 1.1—*cont.*

Before Abrams (the 1950s)	*After Turner (the 1970s)*
2 Conditions for success: self-help reduces costs under all conditions.	2 Conditions for success: self-help increases investment when (a) families have to wait more than five or six years for conventional rental or ownership housing; (b) families find currently available conventional neighbourhoods do not meet their definition of desirable housing.
3 Problems to overcome: (a) lack of land; (b) lack of credit to buy standard materials for a complete house at the date of occupancy; (c) lack of planning and construction skills needed to build conventionally.	3 Problems to overcome: (a) lack of secure, good, well-located building sites; (b) building and land use regulations make a number of self-help options illegal; (c) lack of public services; (d) lack of small construction loans.
4 Solutions: plan house construction to use as much unpaid labour as possible, with appropriate assistance.	4 Solutions: plan new neighbourhoods in which families have secure, good well-located sites, infrastructure and access to technical assistance, and in which families can invest as much or as little as they want. Upgrade old neighbourhoods.
5 Minimum role of government: (a) develop land and infrastructure; (b) design houses; (e) buy materials; (d) organize and supervise construction.	5 Minimum role of government: (a) secure land and develop infrastructure.
6 Ideal project: aided self-help, complete housing scheme.	6 Ideal project: varies with local conditions.
7 Result: high standard housing accessible to low-income families because it is inexpensive.	7 Result: a large number of units varying in cost, and accessible to low-income families because (a) there are enough units; (b) the least costly have secure land, infrastructure and affordable house standards.

redefine self-help, as seen by all of us outside squatter housing, to comprise two elements:

1 Direct investments by families, either unpaid labour or cash savings or, as in the virtually standard squatter neighbourhoods, both of these.
2 Families making decisions.

Like traditional self-help, then, contemporary self-help refers to a form of social decision-making about construction rather than to a particular technological ingredient in the assembly of building components into houses. As such, sites and services and upgrading fall within the self-help housing category. The table (pp. 10–11) outlines the principal differences between the concepts of self-help in the 1950s and after 1970.

Housing policy, therefore, has two quite distinct models of self-help it can follow. How self-help programmes work depends to a large extent on which model policy-makers try to implement. For example, do policy-makers ask for quick production of high-standard housing, relying on intensive use of family labour added to large materials loans, house plans, and instruction in building skills? Or, do they ask for a varied stock of self-help housing in the contemporary sense, and direct the finance from materials loans and technical assistance into extra land and infrastructure? In upgrading, do governments ask for expensive redevelopment of old neighbourhoods or focus on catching up on general provision of infrastructure? And, in both new and old neighbourhoods, how should an agency work with residents – guiding their participation, or adapting itself to community demands?

1.4 Habitat

Neither the two models of self-help nor their distinctive policy implications have been clearly distinguished in policy statements. At the United Nations Conference on Human Settlements (the Habitat Conference) held in Vancouver in 1976, expert delegations representing 124 of the 137 participating governments endorsed a sweeping set of recommendations for national action in settlement policies.

The Habitat resolution (United Nations 1976: 12; all page references in this section refer to this publication) stressed the need for policy to 'focus on the central role of human resources as an agent for development'. Its authors, and presumably the 124 governments who endorsed it, clearly had in mind a decision-making model. Among its specific recommendations (here paraphrased and edited for reasons of brevity), the resolution said:

1 Planning and planners should be brought into close contact with the people especially with respect to the expressed aspirations of the poor and the potential for self-determination (p. 22).
2 Communities should be involved in the planning, implementation and management of neighbourhood schemes (p. 32).
3 Standards for shelter, infrastructure and services should be based on the felt needs and priorities of the population (p. 41).
4 Legislative, institutional and financial measures should be reoriented to facilitate people's involvement in meeting their own needs for social services (p. 55).
5 Public participation is a right of everyone and special efforts should be made to expand and strengthen the role of community organizations, workers' organizations, tenants' and neighbourhood organizations (p. 76).

It has become apparent since Habitat that the general orientation embodied in these policies is not everywhere practical.

Partly the reason lies in national politics where attempts to bring families into planning their own housing uncovers deep conflicts of interest. The Philippines government, for example, which for the duration of Habitat jailed a group of neighbourhood activists wishing to attend the conference, is unlikely to 'strengthen the role of community organizations' based on the principle that 'public participation is a right of everyone' (see also Pincher 1977). Since decision-making does not exist in abstract, someone must work out, as the Habitat resolution (p. 78) says, 'what people can decide and do better themselves' and determine 'the area of government action accordingly'. But the criteria for this is not always a technical one because participation implies a degree of control over public resources, and a corresponding loss of power by agencies that now have this control.

Habitat's policy recommendations also contain internal inconsistencies. The call for measures 'to facilitate people's involvement in meeting their own needs for social services' is juxtaposed to the policy of providing 'social services on an integrated basis' (p. 55). Presumably integrated provision entails a high degree of central co-ordination and decision-making, and it is difficult to see how this would involve self-help except in so far as residents would volunteer for work in what the resolution calls multi-purpose service centres.

Countries that tried to implement some of the Habitat proposals have found such inconsistencies in practice. In Thailand's slum upgrading programme, for example, there is a definite interest amongst certain officials at the project level to see community involvement in neighbourhood management. But success in devising strategies of participation in implementation has been rather uneven, and the involvement of residents has to date been meagre. Since it is unlikely that people will wish to manage (or maintain) that which they do not want and have had no part in designing or implementing, the participatory management attempt is almost bound to fail. Here interdependency of project stages is coupled with a divorce in approach between planners, project teams and 'estate managers'. The last group, in this case, are presented with a 'final product' and with this a project team has to attempt to stimulate participation. Similarly, some of the project team (notably social workers in the Thai case) are struggling to induce residents' involvement in implementation of project components already delivered to the community, with little or no consultation. Until there is an internal co-ordination of planner, project team and management department, and residents, the practical scope for participation is severely limited. What has been said here of Thailand can, of course, equally be said of many other countries.

The Habitat vision of self-help presupposes a more or less rapid coincidence of several, separately unlikely events. General acceptance of the principle and the practice must be matched with new professional competence, with new 'legislative, institutional and financial measures', and with universal organization among poor families for group decision-making. The lack of any one part, even if the rest are in place, can bring the whole effort to a standstill.

What can we conclude from this brief discussion of the Habitat resolution? The resolution is significant because it reveals from an official viewpoint very difficult problems governments in the early 1970s were trying to resolve when changing from conventional to self-help housing policies. By then the reality that self-help meant more than a cheap source of labour was not in question, but the alternative, that families make decisions, was still an unfamiliar and in many ways an uncomfortable alternative. Consequently, while endorsing self-help in abstract, the official view tended to revert to family labour as the starting-point for designing specific proposals. Creating programmes that sanction decisions by families implies that agencies sacrifice some of the nominal powers they are accustomed to and that politically powerful interest groups accept a realignment of their old influence.[1] Such changes seldom occur all at once or, even less seldom, simply by a single restructuring of housing policy. Finally, we have argued that self-help policies create their own special problems of co-ordination among agencies and between agencies and families.

1.5 The following chapters

We have chosen the essays in this volume to begin to fill a gap in the literature on contemporary housing policy. The literature now contains a number of general overviews and technical treatises on various aspects of project planning (Caminos and Goethart 1978; Drakakis-Smith 1981; Dwyer 1975; Shankland Cox Partnership 1977; Wegelin *et al.* 1983; World Bank 1978 and 1981) and a growing volume of work discussing where self-help programmes fit in the social context of Third World countries (Ward 1982, and references therein). In between, however, there is a lacuna in which first, we feel, there is a need to review how different types of programmes have fulfilled expectations (cf. Madavo *et al.* 1978): how, for example, programmes oriented more by the labour model fared in comparison to programmes designed with the decision-making model of self-help in mind. Second, there is a need to see what sort of problems, aside from bad luck and general scarcity of resources, impede implementation of self-help programmes.

Governments have not found self-help policies easy to implement, though the tasks of installing a new water pipe and developing open plots would seem simple in comparison to complete urban renewal and conventional housing estates. Where then are the difficulties?

The next chapter by Rodell examines sites and services, and it maintains that quite a few sites and services programmes in the 1960s and 1970s tried the self-help-equals-family-labour model, and tried to organize family participation along this line. This proved impractical – the programmes actually functioned more according to the family-decision-making-and-direct-investment model of self-help – but it also imposed costs on residents which excluded poorer families. At the same time, decisions about gross density and infrastructure standards resulted in a scarcity of plots, a tendency to locate projects where poorer families could not afford to live, despite low plot prices, and higher rates of subsidy than are feasible for large-scale implementation. Given these tendencies, sites and services, with few exceptions, have not increased the supply of housing for low-income families. Guhr, in chapter 4, tells a similar story about housing co-operatives in Tanzania's sites and services programme. There were, in this case, attempts to create a legal and financial framework to facilitate co-operatives, but institutional infighting and malco-ordination combined with a divergence between family and state-sponsored aims and modes of decision-making rendered the programme ineffective.

Richard Martin's discussion in chapter 3 focuses on how families and planners work out plans for upgrading. He argues the usual prescriptions (e.g. as in the Habitat resolution) for due consultation and for letting families and planners each make decisions within their own respective spheres of competence lead from manipulation and misunderstanding eventually to the concrete result that agencies cannot do much upgrading. Based on his own work in Lusaka, he explains in detail what he calls the bottom-up approach, which essentially is a process of negotiation among residents and between residents and planners. He also makes a case for placing official authority for upgrading in the hands of local governments where families are likely to have the greatest political influence over formulation of policies and approval of projects.

Chapter 7 compares the ways upgrading programmes in four Asian countries have dealt with tenure, standards and subsidies. The author, Paul Baross, contrasts the orthodox formula for upgrading – a project with tenurial security, infrastructure, cost recovery to finance further projects – with Asian practices, and finds the formula wanting. Indigenous customary and market landholding systems do not lend themselves to formalizing individual tenure, and if agencies link tenure to cost recovery they find that residents who effectively, if not legally, control the land do not want upgrading. Often infrastructure goes ahead before there is any resolution of the tenure and subsidy issues. The project approach, however, creates little islands where people effectively pay, and can see that they pay, more than their neighbours pay for public services, which naturally creates opposition that makes projects impractical. Because of this, Baross suggests, large-scale upgrading depends on bringing infrastructural upgrading within the normal budgets for public works and there addressing the subsidy question on a city-wide scale.

Chapter 5 by Emiel Wegelin looks at the elements of self-help programmes and phases of planning and implementation in terms of the governmental and international agencies involved. Like Baross, Wegelin draws on experience in Asia, but he focuses on institutional bottlenecks and sources of institutionalized opposition to effective policies. He expands on the theme of chapter 2 that officials designing programmes have tended to build in barriers to self-help along with supportive, enabling features, owing to long-held opinions that self-help does not contribute positively to housing supply. Vested interests in the construction industry reinforce this view. These interests, according to Wegelin, do not want to see governments directing their budgets away from conventional projects and the lucrative contracts such projects offer. In addition, governmental agencies do not have either enough staff or professionals who are trained to handle new planning and implementation tasks. There are, however, countervailing trends. International agencies played a crucial part in initiating sites and services and upgrading and experimenting with organizational reforms. More important, now, the results of early projects have created awareness of problems and, a vital factor, popular political support for continuing self-help policies.

Skinner, in chapter 6, examines self-help at the collective level, be it in upgrading or sites and services. Many governments attempted to implement the participatory themes of the Habitat resolution, but without the expected results. Part of the problem was a lack of co-ordination in national policies. In Peru, for instance, community organizations were officially welcomed while supporting legislation giving these organizations authority was not passed. Skinner examines a case where a new clinic operated by a community group eventually had to close because of this. Other constraints originated in the way implementing agencies tried to organize participation, and chapter 6 proposes several ways to overcome these constraints. Finally, Skinner confronts the dilemma between the intensive work necessary for successful participation at the project level and the need for extensive implementation of projects. He suggests its resolution lies in viable community organizations themselves. They would, in the figurative sense, repay the investment in their creation by assuming functions a public agency would otherwise have to perform, but for this the organizations have to be vested with genuine authority and not just added costs.

The concluding chapter turns to the future of low-income housing in self-help programmes. Patrick Crooke observes that gradual construction and self-help have indeed, as he puts it, 'exploded' the conventional housing package into pieces, and this has made it possible for a vast array of actors, not only government agencies, to invest in housing. As the resulting increase in housing production enters the market, however, poor families often lose out. This is perhaps the most important issue facing policy-makers in the 1980s. Contemporary policies depend on the market, to be precise on incorporating and supporting the informal market for housing investment, which thus ties the products to market allocation. Crooke formulates the issue succinctly: 'how can governmental supports for popular housing develop in ways which make use of the undoubted efficiencies of the housing market without providing, in the long term, further opportunities for this market to exploit the urban poor?' His answer is that larger scale implementation and revising certain controls over self-help which were part of the 1970s' programmes are necessary but not sufficient; in addition, he argues, future policies would need new systems of land ownership in public projects.

To summarize: self-help housing and policies, in the broadest senses of these terms, are by no means recent inventions or the exclusive province of the Third World. The following essays deal with only selected parts of the total global and historical experience (specifically with policies in Third World cities) that sanction a large role of individual families and community groups in making decisions about their own housing. Policies, like those in Cuba, where government effectively organizes factory workers in construction and limits families' non-labour role to consultative meetings thus fall outside the scope of this volume. Self-help hereafter refers to situations in which direct day-by-day control by families accompanies their actual contribution of resources to house construction, and those situations in which families' political influence necessarily affects planning of infrastructure, facilities, cost recovery systems, and other communal components in the package of housing policy. Self-help of this sort is embodied today in sites and services and upgrading programmes. Self-help policies generally get more self-help than anticipated, because families tend to decide to do things policy-makers did not expect and often may not like.

Sites and services and upgrading, we presume, aim at improving access by poor families to housing of a standard they otherwise would not enjoy. Families' own self-help investment contributes to this aim by enabling governments to plan less of their own investment per unit and to plan more units. In countries where the housing subsidy and self-help together are too small fully to meet housing needs, raising access then requires low standards in projects or gradual construction of infrastructure and facilities, or both. Access might also require low subsidy rates to increase public investment.

The housing thus produced invariably becomes part of a housing market in which, at least now and for the foreseeable future, there is no effective governmental control over ultimate allocation and competitive (sometimes black market) prices. Access in a sites and services or an upgrading project depends not only on whether poor people can afford to pay official prices, but also on whether they can afford to forgo gains from reselling or pay rent increases that follow upgrading. It follows that if policy is to achieve improved low-income access to standards in projects above those prevailing in slum and squatter housing markets, government must flood the market.

Self-help in its economic and its political manifestations, limited subsidies and indigenous housing markets are presently the main constraint on contemporary housing policies in Third World cities. How well the types of self-help programmes planned in the 1970s have adapted to these constraints is a question we hope this book begins to answer in some small measure.

Notes

1 This rests upon our belief that no project is necessarily beneficial to one or other social group or even the government. Much will depend on the design of the project: larger core houses in a sites and services scheme are more likely to satisfy contractors' interests, and land purchase at market rates and thus necessarily subsidized sales to the poor may be advantageous to landowning interests. Larger core houses tend to keep the lower-income groups out of projects, however, because of their costs, and a subsidy policy entails a drain on government revenue. If, then, governments place priority upon low-income access to plots (e.g. for political reasons) or upon tight budgetary control, then the interests of powerful political groups, as here represented by contractors and landowners, may have to be sacrificed. It is the ability to determine which governmental priorities and business interests are dominant or in the ascendancy which will give the project designer the 'room for manoeuvre' referred to in the text.

References

Abrams, C. (1964) *Housing in the Modern World: Man's Struggle for Shelter in an Urbanizing World*, London, Faber & Faber.

Angel, S. and Phoativongsacharn, Z. (1981) *Building Together. Issues in Mutual-Aid Housing*, Bangkok, Asian Institute of Technology, Human Settlements Division, April.

Burgess, R. (1982) 'Self-help housing advocacy: a curious form of radicalism. A critique of the work of John F. C. Turner', in P. Ward (ed.), *Self-Help Housing. A Critique*, London, Mansell, pp. 55–97.

Caminos, H. and Goethart, R. (1978) *Urbanization Primer*, Cambridge, Mass., MIT Press.

Drakakis-Smith, D. (1981) *Urbanization, Housing and the Development Process*, London, Croom Helm.

Dwyer, D. (1975) *People and Housing in Third World Cities*, London, Longman.

Engels, F. (1975) *The Housing Question*, Moscow, Progress Publishers.

Madavo, C., Haldane, D. and Cameron, S. (1978) 'Site and services and upgrading: a review of World Bank-assisted projects', paper presented to the Symposium on the Reduction of Housing Costs, Salvador, Brazil, March.

Pincher, M. (1977) 'Squatters, planning and politics in Tondo, Manila', in Asian Bureau Australia, *Newsletter*, no. 32.

Shankland Cox Partnership (1977) *Third World Urban Housing. Aspirations, Resources, Programmes, Projects*, Watford, Building Research Establishment.

Turner, J. (1976) *Housing by People*, London, Marion Boyars.

United Nations (1976) *Report of Habitat – United Nations Conference on Human Settlements*, New York, United Nations.

Ward, P. M. (ed.) (1982) *Self-Help Housing: A Critique*, London, Mansell.

Wegelin, E. A., Komol Panchee, and Swann, P. (1983) *Management of Sites and Services Housing Schemes*, Chichester, Institute for Housing Studies, John Wiley.

World Bank (1975) 'Sites and services and upgrading, a review of Bank-assisted projects', Washington DC, World Bank, Urban Projects Department.

World Bank (1981) *The Bertaud Model*, Washington DC, Urban Development Department Technical Paper No. 2, prepared by PADCO, Inc., in collaboration with the World Bank staff.

2
Sites and services and low-income housing

M. J. RODELL

2.1 Introduction

This essay is concerned with how effectively sites and services adds to the housing stock and, so far, has succeeded in improving housing for low-income families in Third World cities. Governments can develop between two and five sites and services plots with the resources needed to build a single house in a conventional housing project. On most of the plots, eventually, they can expect houses at least as good as the ones built by public agencies. These two features of sites and services become important advantages in countries with a persistent and general shortage of urban housing, where current construction costs and housing budgets imply, in the face of the rapidly growing need, a large housing gap for several decades.

The inability of conventional housing programmes to meet housing needs follows from the way such programmes concentrate the use of resources and the problems this causes when a large section of a country's population does not yet have standard shelter. The size of the housing stock itself partly determines the savings available for conventional construction. In a country with a large stock, mortgage and rent payments usually provide the bulk savings that pay for new units. Governmental subsidies supplement this, and the subsidies come from taxes, which, like mortgage and rent payments, are paid mainly by families who already have housing. Such countries typically build five to ten houses a year per thousand population (Burns and Grebler 1977: 5). Countries with relatively small housing stocks, with the greatest need, build new units at an annual rate in the range of two to four per thousand population. The funds from mortgage and rent payments, supplemented by subsidies, will not support more than this. And the strategy of conventional construction, which is to collect and concentrate savings from dozens of families with housing, to extend credit or finance subsidies to build a single new house, inevitably means long waiting lists and people having to find shelter in slums and squatter neighbourhoods.

 ## 2.2 Gradual construction and self-help

In a conventional housing project, a contractor completes the investment before families move in. The eventual occupants may pay up to a quarter of the investment costs with a down payment in the case of housing sold on mortgage and hire-purchase contracts. But most of the initial finance necessarily comes from other sources. Then, as the residents repay their loans or pay rent, they provide a small part of the funds every year to build a house for some other family. Both the initial savings for down payments and the subsequent, periodical instalments depend on the physical availability of completed houses.

Sites and services differs from conventional housing in two ways. First, families who move into a sites and services neighbourhood receive only incomplete housing. They may get just land and water in a minimum project, or these with other utilities and core houses in an expensive project. But whatever the type of sites and services, it means a degree of gradual construction of infrastructure or houses, or both, with a significant amount of total investment left until after occupancy.

Second, families in sites and services invest directly in their own housing, rather than pay for something decided and provided by someone else. Self-help, the direct investment by families, can take the form of either labour of family members and friends or purchased materials and hired labour, or a combination of both. This variety of forms of self-help distinguishes sites and services not only from conventional construction, but also from what we might call conventional self-help, in which mainly family labour replaces paid labour in an otherwise conventional construction process. Self-help in sites and services comes closer to its most common form, as seen in the complete planning and organization of housing production by families in squatter neighbourhoods, where the functions of planning and financing are at least as important as family labour.

There is a common impression that both gradual construction and self-help reduce housing costs, and this is why a housing agency, with a given budget, can settle more families in sites and services than in conventional housing estates. This supposition, though, rests on rather imprecise theoretical reasoning. Saying that gradual construction reduces housing costs is analogous to saying that because tyres cost less than a whole car, making initially only tyres reduces the costs of transportation. Perhaps a production process that starts with large-scale development of land and infrastructure achieves certain economies compared to one that starts with the more complicated task of complete housing. Or possibly the phasing of investment in gradual construction might add to costs because some of the tasks, for example, grading roads, have to be repeated over time. No one knows the long-run cost implications of gradual construction. At present, the assumption that total costs, whether investment is phased or whether it is completed before occupancy, will be roughly the same seems just as reasonable as any alternative.

Similarly, we have little empirical basis for sound comparisons between the costs of self-help and conventional housing. Several measurement problems have to be resolved before we do. Because families tend to build gradually and sometimes start with temporary materials, less space, and designs that they eventually replace, the initial costs of a self-help house and its final costs will differ. The latter is the one to be compared to the costs of conventional housing. Ideally, the comparison should distinguish cost variations due to differences in technical efficiency from those that represent differences in standards. For example, families might build larger houses than would an agency, or waste more materials during construction, both of which would tend to make self-help more costly than conventional construction, but with much different implications for planning and evaluating the two modes of production. The most serious measurement problem, however, is how to evaluate the unpaid family labour used in self-help.

The gradual construction and self-help in sites and services projects may or may not, in themselves, significantly alter production costs, though most probably sites and services brings cost reductions because agencies or families decide to lower standards relative to the levels agencies maintained previously in their conventional projects. This is an issue separate from the effects of gradual construction and largely separate from the effects of self-help.[1] Gradual construction accelerates the rate of housing starts in public projects by diverting funds that would be used to complete infrastructure and houses in conventional projects into extra land and infrastructure in sites and services projects. Self-help, in contrast, works much like down payments work in conventional schemes. The greater the proportion of total costs that residents contribute directly, the larger the number of units governments' direct share[2] of costs can finance in a given period of time. In their separate ways, gradual construction and self-help can extend public investments and housing subsidies to a large number of families.

2.3 Planning projects

None the less, governments shifted from conventional to sites and services projects with some reluctance. While the experience of conventional housing's persistent failures and the mounting fiscal problems and growing budgetary demands of social services other than housing provided compelling motives for the changes, sites and services was not a particularly appealing alternative. It abandoned the large subsidies per dwelling and immediately visible, substantial buildings produced by conventional programmes, which had important symbolic value as evidence of modernization and tangible signs of governmental concern for welfare. A large body of professional opinion questioned whether sites and services could achieve any real improvements. It seemed unlikely, in this view, that families gained much by receiving incomplete housing, or that poor families could build decent houses on their own. The working of sites and services ran counter to the long-accepted premise of housing policies − that government had to provide low-income housing because poorer families could not afford to pay the costs of high standards. Self-help threatened to turn public projects into planned slums.

A few countries set up programmes that involved large degrees of gradual construction and self-help, allowing families a wide range of choice over their direct investments and final housing standards. Malawi's traditional housing areas followed this approach. Malawi Housing Corporation laid out plots, built unpaved roads, and installed communal standpipes and water mains that would allow individual connections later. Families could get a small materials loan, or, if they wished, avoid this by starting with traditional, cheaper materials. But most countries' sites and services did not shift this far away from conventional construction. In Tanzania, for instance, plot leases required families to build expensive core houses within six months of allocation or give up their plots. A family could use a plan supplied by the housing bank, or pay a professional designer to prepare an alternative that satisfied the same materials standards as the bank's plans. The building regulations adopted in the Tanzanian programme called for materials costing, at official prices, between one and one-and-a-half times the annual cash incomes of eligible families, thus restricting the degree of gradual construction. To finance the materials and subsidize the programme, both necessary as in conventional programmes because of the low degree of gradual construction, government offered low interest, long-term loans, which in principle were optional, but in practice were mandatory to satisfy the building standards within the six month building limit.

The Tanzanian programme was typical in that its design carefully circumscribed self-help and gradual construction. While agencies relaxed building codes to permit incomplete houses, and simplified house plans to facilitate use of unskilled labour, the plans still tended to require a large part of final infrastructure and houses to be built before occupancy. Some countries tried, like Tanzania, to extend self-help into this initial investment period. The Tanzanian loans and plans assumed the use of family members' own labour. Other countries provided contractor-built core houses instead, and counted on families for finishing and extending dwellings. The relaxation of regulations and simplification of house plans, though, stopped short of allowing the use of temporary materials or traditional construction.

Housing agencies had four main tools for planning self-help projects. First was the construction of core houses and infrastructure. Second were regulations, in the form of norms and of lease and purchase agreements that stipulated what and when families should build. Third was technical assistance (i.e. demonstration houses, house plans, training in building skills and supervision). And fourth was credit and access to building materials via loans, grants and building stores with preferential prices and rations of scarce materials. Plans for sites and services integrated these tools into a system for implementing agencies' ideas. And the plans started with assumptions that self-help should be limited to family labour and that planners should make the main choices about materials, house designs, and the phasing of investment. The flexibility of investment that marks self-help housing outside sites and services was not incorporated. Rather than trying to provide inputs into self-help construction, agencies tried to incorporate unpaid family labour into projects that emulated conventional projects as closely as possible.

Core houses built directly by an agency or by families, plans supplied by an agency, materials standards decided by planners and credit and technical assistance from the government all aimed at the same sort of standards as in conventional housing. Because of this primary concern with standards, the plans excluded a large range of housing options. Families, for example, could not choose to build large houses by economizing on materials initially and gradually substituting better materials later. Furthermore plans prefixed the scheduling of a large part of families' housing costs, either in terms of a large number of hours of labour during a short period of time, or in terms of long-term debt and plot payments near the affordable limits, or both. Consequently, sites and services programmes tended to have only moderate degrees of gradual development and self-help.

Plate 2.1 Arumbakkam project, Madras. Three basic core units and wet cells, available for occupancy in late 1980.

Plate 2.2
Arumbakkam project,
Madras. A house built
on a core unit, March
1981.

Plate 2.3 Sinza project, Dar es Salaam, June 1981. A house started with a self-help construction loan in 1976. Tanzanian materials shortages in the late 1970s meant that standards requiring the use of unavailable materials combined with the project's poor location to produce many units similar to this one.

Plate 2.4 Rangsit project, Bangkok, April 1981. At the date this picture was taken, the project, which was ready for occupancy in 1975, still had about 200 of its 1400 units standing empty, in large measure because of the project's poor location.

27

Plate 2.5 Ibn Khaldoun, Tunis 1981. In the foreground, one of the project's core houses converted into a workshop. In the background, houses families built without following approved designs for extensions.

2.4 Self-help investment

Given the initial scepticism about self-help and the subsequent attempts carefully to limit the scope of self-help in sites and services, it is not surprising that most studies of programmes addressed this issue.[3] They have so far asked global questions: do families invest a lot in housing? Do they build good houses? Do they follow plans and invest mainly their own labour? Yes, it most often happens that families do invest, and do build good houses, but they frequently do not follow plans. Other important issues have only begun to receive attention. Evaluation studies have not compared self-help inside projects with self-help in squatter neighbourhoods, or examined the ways that the tools for planning self-help worked.

Scattered evidence suggests that the plans for self-help did not work well. First of all, the integrated systems of controls tended to involve families in bureaucratic tangles. Tanzania's, for example, tied tenure to construction of a core house requiring a bank loan and building approval. Loan applications and building approval forms had to pass through several offices in the housing bank and the city administration, which in many cases took longer than the six months that lease agreements allowed for completion of the core house. Families who waited for a loan and approval violated their leases; families who started without a loan and approval violated their leases. In principle, both groups could have lost their plots had the lease provisions been implemented according to plan.

Once a family secured a loan, it faced even more severe problems. Economy-wide shortages of approved building materials, cement in particular, prevented families completing their core units and using their loans in full. Cement was not available at the official prices used to calculate loan amounts, so in practice, the loans did not buy as much cement as planners had assumed. Since the bank disbursed the loans in stages, each stage depending on successful completion of the preceding one, when the funds from the initial disbursal did not complete the first stage, families had to either stop construction or save and spend their own funds.

Materials shortages plagued sites and services everywhere, but most severely in Africa. Robertson (1978) estimated that Zambian stocks of roofing sheets were enough for only one-fourth of all new houses planned in urban areas during the middle and late 1970s. Because official standards did not allow other materials for roofing in sites and services, families were forced to choose between not following plans or not building.

A number of experimental projects tried to overcome the shortage of materials by using innovative building systems in which self-help played a role in materials production as well as in building. The Chawama self-help housing project in Kafue, Zambia, developed one of the more successful of such systems, saving costs of cement by using stabilized soil blocks for walls (AFSC 1975). The planners of the project credit it with providing better houses than could have been built by families on their own, a conclusion supported by independent observers (Martin 1975: 121). Yet, what is not clear from Chawama, or in similar projects elsewhere, is the extent to which self-help contributes to success.

For Chawama, Kafue City Council granted the land, provided part of the office space and administration, and with a grant and a low-interest loan from central government installed the infrastructure. Central government gave residents small, low-interest loans for building materials and grants for sanitary installations. Non-governmental organizations donated money and equipment, and paid the professional staff who designed the houses and played a large role in managing construction. Families, for their part, bought about half of the materials for the houses, and each put in about 1000 hours of work for a two-room core house. In addition to this direct investment, they repaid the materials loans, and paid regular service charges and taxes.

The substitution of stabilized soil for cement blocks undoubtedly reduced construction costs, and freed the project from delays and stoppages it might have faced had it used more cement. The self-help side of the project, though, was less successful. While it worked, it was also expensive. Family labour replaced an estimated $350 of paid labour per core house. Grants associated with planning and supervising the family labour amounted to between $600 and $700.[4] Grants made up two-thirds of the project's budget and, adding in the land grant, interest rate subsidies, and expenses not charged to the project, subsidies of all forms made up an even larger proportion of total costs. Chawama, moreover, was nearly conventional in its heavy concentration of investment in the period prior to occupancy, in spite of producing incomplete housing with a large degree of self-help. In this case, the attempt to plan self-help sacrificed the advantages of both self-help and gradual construction.

Plans for self-help also encountered open resistance from families in some projects, which is best illustrated by families' efforts to alter the plans. When I visited a Tunisian project, Ibn Khaldoun, some eighteen months after the first families had moved in, in one sector I counted forty core units with modifications and extensions out of a total of sixty. Only one had followed the plan: the Tunisians had provided several types of core house, built by contractors, and each one with its own design for extensions with self-help. The plans in principle left families to decide the phasing of extensions; all other decisions had been made. In practice, however, people have ignored the designs. Not only have they designed their own extensions but in about half the cases I saw they significantly changed the core itself. They moved windows and doors, and in a few cases had even removed external walls to accommodate their plans. From the residents' point of view, much of the investment in the core houses had been wasted, adding both to hire-purchase payments for something families did not use and to costs of construction for the final houses.

The cases discussed here suggest that much of what agencies did to plan self-help investment actually had negative effects. To the extent this reflects the trial and error of first efforts, it is not surprising. Sites and services were launched without a full understanding of what would and would not work. Yet experience indicates that plans for self-help investment also started with faulty assumptions. First, family labour does not, as initially thought, play a dominant role in self-help. In a summary evaluation of its first twenty-six basic urbanization (upgrading and sites and services) projects, the World Bank (1978: 16) found family labour was used mainly for such tasks as clearing plots, finishing work and supervising construction. Between 40 and 80 per cent of families hired small contractors for the main parts of house-building. In a recent survey of twenty-two houses in a Tanzanian project, owners reported building all or mostly by themselves in only three cases (Schilderman 1981: 3). This feature does not seem a special characteristic of self-help in sites and services. The Tanzanian survey, for instance, found in a sample of fifty-six houses in an upgrading and a squatter neighbourhood just nine built all or mostly by their owners.

Second, families do invest a surprisingly large amount of cash savings. They may be spending, in addition to money they borrow, amounts equivalent to 40 per cent of their current cash incomes to buy materials and pay contractors during the year or two after they occupy plots.[5] The largest part of the savings come from current earnings (Magembe 1981), supplemented from other sources (e.g. pensions, sales of houses, sales of businesses, compensation payments and gifts and loans from relatives).

Third, the connection between current cash income and housing investment turns out to be weaker than once thought. Table 2.1 illustrates this with data from an evaluation of Zambian projects. The survey unfortunately recorded only the cash incomes of heads of households, rather than total income from all sources, but it shows direct cash investments by families with earnings above the bottom range are widely dispersed. (For purposes of comparison, Martin's study (1975: 14) mentions a survey of a squatter neighbourhood, in which seven-tenths of household heads earned between 30 and 89 kwacha a month.) A number of factors could explain the variation: differences in the use of hired labour; choices about house sizes, materials, phasing investments; differences in accumulated cash and non-cash savings, as well as differences in income from other sources. Whatever the reasons, plans based on the idea of simple affordability in strict proportion to incomes started with a fundamental misconception about self-help investment.

Finally, and perhaps most important, families plan their own investments and cannot be easily made to follow agencies' plans. This possibility had been a major argument against adopting sites and services, because of the belief that self-help would produce permanently substandard housing out of a chaos of individual decision-making. Planning by families, however, serves several important adaptive functions. Investment capacity varies from family to family, not only in terms of how much each one can invest over a long period, but also in terms of when they can invest. Part of the variation shown in table 2.1 probably reflects this – some families deciding to build more gradually than others – as much as it reflects long-run differences in what people ultimately hope to achieve. Without planning done by the families, there would be no way to adapt the phasing of construction to these differences. A common

Table 2.1 Households classified by investment expenses and income of household head in four Zambian projects, 1974.

Monthly cash income (kwacha)	Direct investment expenses (kwacha)					Total number of households
	Under 150	150– 299	300– 499	500– 999	1000– 1499	
Over 119	1	2	8	8	2	21
90–119	—	2	3	6	—	11
60–89	9	9	11	9	4	42
30–59	29	25	15	6	—	75
Under 30	14	2	—	—	—	16
Unemployed	5	3	5	7	—	20
Total number of households	58	43	42	36	6	185

Source: Adapted from Martin 1975: table 5.1.

schedule would force unwanted hardship on some, and too much, equally unwanted, gradual construction on others.

Investment capacity also varies in terms of how much labour families can afford in relation to the total of their direct investment. Projects that tried, like Chawama, to plan a common schedule or, like Tanzania's sites and services, to concentrate large amounts of family labour into a short period before occupancy, roughly the same for all families, run into 'affordability' constraints for time as severe as the constraint on expenses.

An adaptive function of self-help is equally important in deciding about standards, especially in gradual construction. Plans for self-help tended to economize on room space standards in favour of materials standards. Plans also precluded the use of temporary materials, trying to get families to start with small, high-quality space and maintain the same materials standards throughout the lengthy period of construction. Many families, for as much as a small, standard core would cost initially, need instead extra space rather than the more costly materials. Partly, the concern about the effects of self-help on materials standards has proven misplaced because it was based on an underestimate of what families would save and invest in sites and services.

Self-help's adaptive functions are crucial because in sites and services, unlike in conventional housing, the resources and the final decisions to invest or not rest with individual families. When agencies' plans require investments much different from families' own priorities, the plans can cut off investment. A World Bank evaluation (1978: 16) concluded that plans for co-operative self-help projects have had this effect. Similarly, the costs that modifying Ibn Khaldoun's core houses added to self-help, for example, certainly did not stimulate direct investment by families. The evidence now in hand shows little need for such directive stimulation anyway. Families investments are on average substantial and do produce decent housing (Bamberger 1979: 47; Martin 1975: 54–61; Nathan 1978: 17; World Bank 1978: 17f.). For certain standards, self-help houses tend to exceed the norms of conventional housing projects. Martin (1975: 55ff.), for example, found families in Zambian projects quickly built houses averaging twice the size (number of rooms) of municipal council units. If the families he interviewed realized their plans, average room space per dwelling will exceed three times the official standards. In the Zambian projects, Martin concluded (1975: 119ff.), little that housing agencies did to plan self-help appeared to positively affect either immediate investments or long-run standards of houses.

Indeed, few of the problems of sites and services programmes to date stem from deficiencies of self-help investment. Difficulties lie, instead, in barriers to providing plots on a sufficient scale to reach low-income families.

2.5 Slow plot development

A surprising number of programmes have projects with a high proportion of unoccupied and undeveloped plots. Besides problems of inter-agency conflicts and lack of co-ordination that delay completion of projects (Khan and Mirza 1981; Mghweno and Satyanarayana 1978), relatively high costs to families account for a large part of slow plot development.

The role of official prices appears clearly in Zambian projects, for example, where government has offered relatively expensive standard plots, with initially more complete services and other amenities, and inexpensive basic plots, with less complete services. The idea was to open projects to a wider income group than was thought could afford the standard plots. Yet, studies (Martin 1975: 13) indicate little difference between the incomes of families on the two types of plots. And unpublished reports indicate that sometimes as much as half the standard plots lie idle in projects by the time all the basic plots are inhabited.

Costs to families that are less obvious than plot charges also impede plot development. The high costs of Tanzania's core houses stopped many families' construction. A tour of the Tanzanian projects today shows not only a large proportion of plots without any houses, and loans allocated to buy materials remaining unused, but also a large number of houses standing half finished because of the costs of cement required by standards. The irony in this is that the integrated system of planning self-help to ensure production of good houses has actually stopped self-help and blocked a gradual process of construction that would have produced the wanted houses.

Similar problems follow attempts to keep plot charges low by locating projects on cheap land. The narrow view of housing costs that counts only development expenses fails to appreciate that plot charges families save because they live on cheap land may be more than offset by added commuting costs arising from poor location. A Tanzanian family with the minimum wage in the late 1970s would have had to spend 10–20 per cent of its income on bus fares if it lived in a sites and services project and could not walk to work. This, added to the 20–25 per cent that was planned for plot charges and loan repayments, not counting what the family would spend to complete its housing, would have brought housing costs up to 45 per cent of monthly income – two to five times more than families paid in squatter neighbourhoods.[6]

Poor location, of course, means sites located beyond the commuting distances to major concentrations of jobs. Attempts to solve this problem without reducing density and infrastructural standards have concentrated on moving jobs out to sites and services projects, by adding land and buildings for businesses. Unfortunately, it is often as difficult to find firms willing to work at chosen locations as it is to find families for the plots, and the employers that do move to projects may not solve the problem. Existing businesses relocating their operations bring along a large part of the work force, normally as commuters and not as residents. Relocating firms thus do not provide a large employment base for speedy plot development. New firms tend not to offer a large enough number or the right range of jobs.

Much less a large programme of sites and services, even single projects with special advantages face this problem. Dasmarinas, a project on the periphery of Manila (Lazaro and Lingan 1981), was located in a zone where the metropolitan master plan had excluded industrial activities. The project received a variance from the zoning restriction in the hope that it would be able to attract firms and match jobs with houses. The project in effect held a complete monopoly on industrial sites in a large sector of Manila, and consequently easily found industries willing to set up plants on the site. In 1979, about five years after development started, the project had succeeded in creating 1900 industrial jobs inside, and 4600 other jobs. Still, about 680 people, less than 10 per cent of the residents' labour force, worked in Dasmarinas (Lazaro and Lingan 1981: 14).

2.6 Access by low-income families

Slow plot development actually represents just one of the problems caused by poor location. At the extreme, a project may be so far from employment centres that it attracts few families. Projects somewhat better located may attract families, but not from the income group they are designed for. Thailand's National Housing Authority discovered this in its first sites and services project, Rangsit, built in 1977. It was an experimental project, designed to test the workability of sites and services as an alternative to conventional housing for families with incomes less than $75 a month (Somsak and Komson 1981: 15), but it was located on land some two hours by bus from the centre of Bangkok. NHA received just over 200 applications for the project's 1400 plots and core houses. Rather than leave plots empty, it finally decided to open the project to families with incomes above the initial target and, by October 1980, about 1200 families had moved in (Somsak and Komson 1981: 23). During the first three years, 800 of the original plot holders sold their plots, which two of the project's planners attribute to 'the fact that inappropriateness of project location caused more problems . . . than the housing shortage problem itself' (Somsak and Komson 1981: 23).

By mid-1980, according to an unpublished survey by NHA, well over half the households living in Rangsit had incomes exceeding the initially planned maximum. Table 2.2 compares the income distribution of the original 500 plot holders in 1977 with the income distribution of 1200 families in 1980.

While the project did not fully reach the group of families for which it was designed, it did better than sites and services have managed in many countries. Estimates (Thailand 1980: 38) of the income distribution in Bangkok indicate the bottom 30 per cent of families had monthly incomes under $175 in 1980, and three-fourths of the families in Rangsit

Table 2.2   1977 and 1980 income distribution of families in Rangsit.

Reported monthly income (US dollars)	1977	1980
	% of families	
Under 75	24.9	10.9
75–125	35.9	36.1
126–175	22.9	30.1
176–250	12.2	16.9
Over 250	3.8	6.0

Source: Data from surveys by the Estate Management Department, National Housing Authority, Thailand.

fell in this category. In contrast, the World Bank's review of projects in
seventeen countries (1978: 22) concluded sites and services have generally been too expensive for the bottom 20 per cent of families, and 'serve
the upper segment of the . . . groups that can afford them'.

The World Bank's conclusions distinguish between the group that
theoretically can afford sites and services and the group that ends up
living in projects. The first depends on standards and subsidy policies,
and the culprit here is an unwillingness to accept standards that the
poorest fifth of families could afford. On the one hand, the moderate to
low degrees of self-help and gradual development planned in many programmes reflect this. On the other hand, and more fundamentally,
agencies set certain long-run standards (plot sizes, public reservations
and public facilities) that keep costs high regardless of the degree of self-
help or gradual development. Malawi's sites and services, which
represent the extreme possibility of self-help and gradual development,
also have the largest plot sizes of any programme (Crooke 1981: 23).[7]

As yet, planners have no firm guidelines for estimating the affordability of sites and services, and this too has contributed to the tendency
to plan unrealistically high standards and unrealistically low degrees of
gradual development. With conventional housing on rental or purchase
contracts, planners could reasonably approximate how much families
might spend from budget surveys. The nature of sites and services makes
this unworkable. Not only are families buying incomplete housing (so
presumably they can afford less for it than for conventional housing), but
they are also investing. What they can afford for land and services is
likely to increase as they complete their houses. Despite these obvious
differences, planners have tended to apply the same affordability guidelines for both conventional and sites and services projects. In Thailand,
budget surveys indicated that families with around $75 monthly income
spend roughly 20 per cent on housing. This was the figure, $15 per
month, used to plan the Rangsit project (Somsak and Komson 1981).
The second part of the World Bank's distinction − who among those
theoretically able to afford sites and services actually live in projects −
depends largely on the housing market. Official allocation procedures
cannot correct a lack of applications for projects planned at locations far
from jobs or at prices and costs dictated by standards beyond the limits
of low-income demand. When projects such as Rangsit do not compare
favourably, in families' view, with slum and squatter alternatives, lack of
low-income demand leaves plots open only for higher-income groups.
Where agencies have been able to allocate plots according to policy,
voluntary reselling and renting tends to negate the effort. Families have
been able easily to avoid legal restrictions against transfer and when

transfers take place as fast as they did at Rangsit – a turnover of 55 per cent of plots in three years – agencies do not have the personnel to enforce restrictions. Even subsidized prices cannot guarantee access by poor families when richer ones will pay substantial premiums to buy into projects.

The characteristics of demand for sites and services raises questions that strict allocation rules, transfer restrictions, and subsidies alone cannot resolve. Demand so far (World Bank 1978: 13) has been from the third to the sixth deciles of the income distribution. Does this reflect structural features of demand or more the effects of prices and standards programmes offered? Crooke (1981: 18f.) reports surveys in Malawi that found 70–80 per cent of projects' residents were renters, and he attributes this largely to relatively high demand for rental rather than ownership among Malawi's urban low-income families. I found similar evidence that structural features account for part of the discrepancy between planned and actual allocation in Tanzanian projects. In both a sites and services neighbourhood and upgrading and squatter neighbourhoods surveyed in 1981, renters' households averaged half the size of owners', had fewer children, and six times more had no children at all. About 80 per cent of the renters reported no immediate plans to buy or build their own house. Renters reported lower household cash incomes, the variable so far used by planners when measuring access, but, because of the smaller size of households, actually had *per capita* incomes roughly a third higher than owners' households. Possibly, strict allocation rules to direct plots to the bottom of the household income distribution may be misdirected and so there are relatively few takers, while effective restrictions on renting would exclude an important segment of low-income families from the benefits of living in sites and services.

How have prices and standards affected access by poorer families? Besides the universally acknowledged, if not yet firmly defined, relation between price and affordability, prices and standards have important consequences for the scale of sites and services, which may be as important as affordability for reaching poorer families. High initial standards limit the number of plots agencies can provide, and simultaneously attract families with incomes above the median. Subsidies that are then necessary to make high standards affordable by families in the second income decile will be effective only after there are enough plots for the middle-income group. The subsidies, though, further limit plot production and intensify competition from middle-income families, because projects with high subsidy rates return less money for reinvestment than do projects with low rates.

The traditional definition of access as the proportion of families owning plots from the lower third or fifth of income distribution obscures the importance of scale. It would be better to consider the number of lower-income families as the measure of access, recognizing that programmes with a small proportion of low-income families but a large number of plots could increase low-income access more than a programme with a high proportion on few plots. As Patrick Crooke points out in the final chapter of this volume, sites and services programmes have not done well on the number measure. Of the countries discussed here so far, Malawi (Crooke 1981: 15f.) is the only one in which sites and services houses more than 10 per cent of the population in any city. After starting in the 1950s and emphasizing sites and services in the 1970s, the Malawian government had housed over a third of the population in its largest city, and with this had managed to slow the growth of squatter neighbourhoods to the city's average rate of population growth during the last decade. Elsewhere, only a few countries have produced enough plots to appreciably increase housing supply; with the problems of slow plot development, prices and standards, and middle-income competition contributing to the fundamental constraint of small scale, sites and services has not reached, generally, a large proportion of poor families.

2.7 Cost recovery

The imperative for large-scale production as a pre-condition for improving access has made cost recovery an important issue in planning sites and services. One reason for turning from conventional housing was that it not only concentrated subsidies in ways that made large-scale production impossible, but it also had resulted in large, unplanned subsidies. On the one hand, housing agencies owned houses with rising maintenance costs and more or less fixed rental rates; and, on the other hand, the agencies were not collecting the revenues they asked. The possibility to compensate for the growing deficit by increasing grants for maintenance and for debt repayment was not great. Once it was exhausted, agencies reduced maintenance, curtailed further construction to free investment funds for repaying debt, or often both. In short, unplanned subsidies limited the supply of conventional public housing.

Sites and services, largely because it involved home ownership, was supposed to help solve these problems. Home ownership removed from agencies the responsibility for maintaining dwellings, which both eliminated a source of expenditure and reduced a cause of complaints – poor maintenance – that possibly contributed to non-payment of rents. Planners also hoped people would be more willing to pay for the right of ownership than they were for rental accommodation. But if ownership has had any effect at all, it has not prevented the problems of unplanned subsidies carrying over from conventional housing to sites and services.

While we are concerned here with the shortfalls in project revenues, it is worth noting that this is not the only, or always the largest, cause of unplanned subsidies. The accounts of Thailand's Rangsit project, shown in table 2.3, for example, reveal one case where operating cost overruns will eventually account for most of the unplanned subsidies. (The $423,000 loss, made good wholly from grants, in the short period of less than three years could have paid for the materials, labour and equipment for over 180 additional units.) Yet, when maintenance and operating expenses consistently exceed expectations, the reason must lie in the methods planners use to project expenses – most probably in failing to add in expected inflation. The revenue shortfalls are less easily diagnosed.

First, not all revenue shortfalls show up in projects' accounts. This occurs most obviously when co-ordination problems and materials short-ages delay occupancy and the receipt of revenues, but it also happens when agencies postpone, for any reason, the start of revenue collections. While plans are made on the assumption of full occupancy from the time a project is completed, accounts are kept on the basis of revenues due from the date of allocation. Thus when poor location, administrative red tape, or prices delay occupancy, unrecorded revenue losses begin to accumulate. Accounts show only one type of revenue shortfall in the difference between revenues due and receipts, usually lumped together under the heading of combined arrears and defaults, which can seriously misrepresent the true magnitude of shortfalls. Adjusting the accounts in table 2.3 for a seven-months delay in Rangsit's completion (Somsak and Komson, 1981: 20), for instance, would add $150,000 to the revenue

Table 2.3 Revenues and operating budget, Rangsit sites and services project February 1977 to September 1980 (US dollars).

	Planned	Actual	Loss relative to plan
Revenues from monthly payments	740,000	504,000	– 236,000
Maintenance and operating expenses	310,000	733,000	−423,000
Surplus or deficit	430,000	−229,000	−659,000

Source: Data provided by the National Housing Authority, Thailand.

shortfall. Rangsit was fortunate in that it was wholly financed by grants and was a pilot project, since shortfalls totalling some $380,000 in three years on a single project would have seriously reduced the feasible scale of production in a larger programme.

Second, a variety of factors combine to cause large and persistent revenue shortfalls. Residents in Rangsit claimed that when they moved to the project their commuting costs increased so much they often could not meet what had seemed a reasonable payment of $15 per month. Complaints of this sort also occur when agencies do not maintain services, and people object to paying for paved roads with potholes, unreliable water supply, community facilities with closed doors and uncollected garbage. Ironically, the root of dissatisfaction that contributes to arrears and defaults often lies in decisions aimed at increasing low-income access, such as choosing cheap sites and not realistically projecting operating costs.

In self-help projects, agencies' regulatory functions create a second source of dissatisfaction. Again we might note with some irony, that while the general justification for regulations is to ensure poor families have decent housing, the effect often is to close the channels that make improved housing possible through self-help and gradual construction. Enforcement of some regulations, such as those against building space for business or room rentals, reduces incomes and, with incomes, the ability to pay plot charges, loan instalments, and gradually raise dwelling standards. Other regulations threaten the security and willingness to invest of the poorest families who can live in projects. Attempts like Tanzania's to force rapid construction and, simultaneously, expensive materials standards fall in this category. When regulations that already restrict access then damage the interests of residents, this damage provides a motive for non-payment.

Sites and services, especially in programmes financed by the World Bank (1978: 20), have enjoyed a special institutional status that gives a third source of dissatisfaction. The World Bank has made high planned rates of cost recovery one of its criteria for extending loans. Where existing housing institutions did not have the means (e.g. taxes and rates set in proportion to infrastructure and service costs) or the freedom politically to meet the criteria, governments created new agencies or a separate set of regulations just for sites and services projects. Under these special arrangements, governments end up charging residents in projects more for the same or less services than is charged for in other neighbourhoods.

Dissatisfactions about basic design features, about maintenance, about regulations, and about unfair prices add to political pressures against collecting revenues. As representatives of government, agencies often cannot use their formal powers to collect revenues. One official told me that 'nobody loses a promotion because of defaults, but evictions would cause problems'. Occasionally the pressures appear visibly, as they did in Botswana. The sites and services agency in Botswana's capital city had to implement its programmes under a policy of strict cost recovery. Neither the national government, which was trying to end urban subsidies and increase rural subsidies, nor the town council would vote annual subsidies. The agency issued plot holders a perpetual certificate of rights, which had a clause making continued occupation contingent on payment of lease fees. When the agency started to enforce this clause (Foundation for Cooperative Housing *c.* 1980: 22f.), the proportion of families 'in default' (presumably, those who had failed to pay for several months in succession) was high. Social workers visited defaulters to explain the requirement for payment. If this failed, the agency issued notice and eventually evicted families. Under this regime evictions were rare and there 'was a rather immediate improvement in the overall rate of payments'. The town council, however, followed this by issuing new certificates without the eviction clause, after which non-payments returned to their earlier level.

When agencies combine the functions of producer, regulator and governmental representative, the last two bring with them the risk of revenue shortfalls that prevent investment in future projects. Measures to improve collections without altering these functions offer some hope. For example, agencies can avoid discretionary non-payment by collecting instalments through pay-roll deductions. By raising down payments and allotment fees, and correspondingly reducing monthly payments, agencies can lower the amounts lost in arrears and defaults. But these measures, too, have disadvantages. Pay-roll deductions presume a form of employment many low-income families do not have, while large initial payments impede access more than would be necessary if agencies collected at least 90–95 per cent of payments due.

If institutional changes prove to be essential for this and revised measures of collecting revenues can offer limited improvement, the obvious third area of needed change is project design. A remarkable number of design features are implicated in the cost recovery problems – poor location, infrastructure and superstructure that causes delays in land development and plans for self-help – and simultaneously contribute in non-financial ways to slow plot development and access problems. Alterations of the design features would help, on a broad front, to reverse the glum prediction (World Bank 1978: 21) that 'Unless ways can be found to remove constraints to larger scale operations . . . site and services will fail to contribute significantly to the solution of problems precipitated by rapid urbanization.'

2.8 Changes in policies

Up to this point in the essay, I have focused on what might be called early sites and services programmes, or more precisely perhaps, the types of projects taken up most frequently as the next best to conventional housing. These tended to entail low to moderate degrees of gradual construction, with low to somewhat more than moderate degrees of self-help and a variety of controls on families' direct investments. Programmes exemplified by Malawi's open plot subdivisions with high degrees of gradual construction and self-help stood out in sharp contrast to the typical design. My intention was to show that the principal problems in sites and services have little to do with self-help as such, despite planners' and policy-makers' anxiety that it would be the main source of difficulty.

From the early programmes, sites and services started a slow evolution on two distinct lines. Along one, new projects began to shed parts of their predecessors' plans for self-help in favour of allowing increased scope for family decision-making. Clear examples can be seen in Karachi's Metrovilles (Khan and Mirza 1981), which have few building controls, and in Zambia's basic plot programme. An increased degree of gradual construction was adopted partly as an implicit side-effect of greater reliance on family decision-making and partly by reducing initial investments in infrastructure and facilities. Finally, along the first line of evolution, projects started to reflect concessions on standards that, unlike those pertaining to the initial dwelling and infrastructure which can be raised gradually, are more likely to be permanent. This new species of project appeared with reduced public reservations and plot sizes.

A second line of evolution produced projects with numerous plot options in place of one or two types of plots as in almost all early projects. The Arumbakkam project in Madras (Lakshmanan and Kumaresan 1981) offers six types, ranging in area from 40 m² up to 220 m²; Thailand's second sites and services scheme (Seri *et al.* 1981) offers seven types, from an open plot to one with a two-storey semi-detached core house. The project incorporates some features (e.g. relaxed building regulations, open plots, no technical assistance for self-help) of the first line of evolution alongside deliberate differentiation of plots to attract a mix of income groups.

Increasing family decision-making and the degree of self-help, increasing the degree of gradual construction and lowering plot sizes and public reservations obviously aim at reducing costs and standards to make more plots available. The first two work on initial costs and the last on final costs. On the other hand, mixed-income projects lend themselves to several possible aims:

1 By matching plot options closely with demand, projects might reduce middle-income competition for the portion of plots designed for poorer families. Arumbakkam, for instance, offers 40 m² plots that middle-income families most likely do not want, especially when the same project has plots five times larger.
2 By subsidizing less costly plots at a high rate and more costly plots at a low rate, this approach might be able to improve cost recovery. There have been tentative steps toward selling more expensive plots at market prices and actually generating cross-subsidies to finance added land and infrastructure investment.
3 Finally, mixed-income projects can keep more or less the same average standards as in earlier projects. This may be the only way some agencies can win approval for, say, some small plots and relaxed building regulations, while the advertising value of quickly built, substantial houses that middle-income self-help produces insulates a programme from the charge of creating planned slums.

The tendency is to see mixed-income projects as a way to ensure low-income access without sacrificing overall standards, and without additional outside subsidies. The choices among the three tactical aims is at present something of an unrecognized problem in itself.

No doubt the right balance of (a) political necessity (adopting standards higher, and degrees of self help and gradual development lower, than feasible for large-scale development of land), (b) differential subsidy rates, and (c) discriminatory standards is as variable between countries as any planning parameter. But mixed-income projects have rather obvious limitations that can turn the projects into barriers to improving low-income housing.

To planners' great consternation, the mixed-income project does deliberately what the market did in early sites and services: it directs public investment away from low-income families. Whether it works will depend on its increasing access. In the short run, a marked improvement in the percentage of poor families living in projects must occur. Given the proven impotence of subsidized prices to accomplish this, planners will have to place heavy reliance on the first objective mentioned above producing a high proportion of plot options that middle-income families do not want.

In the long run, mixed-income projects must be an effective instrument for increasing public housing investment, so that they offset the lesser investment planned per project for low-income families with larger total investment. Objective 3 can help, perhaps, by creating support and willingness to enlarge grants and enact measures such as land reform for public housing. But the main burden of mobilizing savings lies with housing agencies, and through agencies with the families living in projects. Objective 2, then, is critical for improving access in the long run: differential subsidy rates have to be used to lower the average rate of subsidy.[8] The initial average cost per plot in mixed-income projects tends to be roughly similar to costs in early projects. Planners have kept average standards roughly constant, adding to middle-income plots, infrastructure and facilities what they take away from low-income plots. Not only does this limit the ability to increase access, since agencies can only produce the same number of plots as they could produce with a given budget in early projects, but it runs the risk of mixed-income projects evolving further into even more costly designs, which in the long run will mean fewer, not more, units available.

In a perceptive study of housing standards and prices in Bangkok (Thailand 1980: 37ff.), Thailand's National Housing Authority concludes that the

large difference of income between the theoretical target group and real client group (for mixed-income projects with high average standards) points out . . . a major flaw in housing policy or . . . a mistake in project location, standards, or prices. Pending the subsequent action to remedy this situation by adjusting standards or policy, the real client groups have to be acknowledged, and designs eventually modified to fit more closely [their] requirement[s].

The study quite explicitly delineated what it meant by 'theoretical target' and 'real client' groups: the former comprised all families who could afford one or more of the plot options provided in NHA's second sites and services project (planned for two-thirds occupancy by families in the second and third deciles of the income distribution), while the latter was families in the fourth to seventh deciles.

Agencies can follow NHA's advice by raising standards to provide units and neighbourhoods more in line with the middle-income ideal. Then costs will escalate, and possibilities for differential subsidization will soon reach a limit (one reason why middle-income families have housing problems is that they, too, cannot afford to pay unsubsidized prices for conventional housing). One can predict that agencies following this approach will eventually reduce the degrees of gradual development and self-help in their projects. An increasing proportion of public investment will go into core houses, complete infrastructure, and large loans for house-building. One can also predict, if less confidently, that large plots and large public reservations, nearly complete core houses and complete infrastructure, substantial long-term construction loans and amenities will necessitate large subsidies per middle-income family. Along this path, sites and services does not have far to go before its initial investment per family and the long-run restriction on investment funds imposed by subsidized prices make it a negligible source of low-income housing.

Alternatively, agencies can follow NHA's advice by providing the minimum initial investment needed to attract middle-income families. This strategy was followed in Madras's Arumbakkam project. In addition to complete infrastructure networks and other amenities, very little beyond land was designed for middle-income families. The top three plot options (see table 2.4) had neither core houses or construction loans, nor water or sewerage connections. Rather than modifying design toward less self-help and gradual development, Arumbakkam's planners adopted more of both for its higher options, and relied on plot size and common amenities as sufficient attractors. By the time the project delivered its final plots in April 1980, it appeared to have successfully reconciled its theoretical target and real client groups without excessive concentration of its resources for middle-income housing (table 2.5).

The data in table 2.5 suggests that a single project like Arumbakkam might be subject to some resale to higher than intended income groups.

Table 2.4 Plot options in Arumbakkam, design and allocation parameters.

Plot option	area (m²)	% of residential land	On-plot development service connections	Structure (m²)	Theoretical target group (percentile of the income distribution)
A	40.0	35.6	yes	3.5	9–19
B	46.5	18.1	yes	18.5	20–44
C	46.5	7.3	yes	28.5	45–57
D	74.3	19.9	no	none	58–71
E	139.4	21.6	no	none	72–81
F	223.0	19.1	no	none	82–94

Sources: The last column is derived from an unpublished internal memorandum, Madras Metropolitan Development Authority. All other columns from Lakshmanan and Kumaresan (1981: 12).

Note: About two-thirds of the population, or 60 per cent of the families in Madras according to official estimates, fall in the category of 'incomes below the survival level' (i.e. *per capita* cash incomes less than $8 per month in the mid-1970s).

Table 2.5 Arumbakkam: initial demand.

Plot option	% of plots	Number of plots	Number of applications	Number of eligible applications	% of eligible applications
A	45.6	1058	839	839	20.4
B	20.1	462	1690	1336	32.6
C	7.8	179	1380	625	15.3
D	13.8	319	699	452	11.0
E	8.0	184	883	631	15.5
F	4.4	102	351	212	4.2

Source: See table 2.4.

Specifically, there was a large excess demand for the middle range of plot options, and a disproportionately large demand by ineligible − middle-income − families for option C. But the frequency distribution of demand also leaves room for cautious optimism that a programme of similar projects could attract and keep enough low-income families to begin to improve the supply of housing for this group.

A comparison of tables 2.4 and 2.5, finally, serves to stress the dangers in the mixed-income approach. The top plot option, F, accounted for only 4.4 per cent of the units, though producing it absorbed nearly 20 per cent of the project's net residential land. Had Arumbakkam chosen the alternative of building core units or supplying construction loans with the top plots the concentration of investment would have been much greater than it was, and the number of plots for low-income families much lower. It is this type of concentration of initial investments on a few families that threatens most the chance low-income families have of ever living in sites and services. If we imagine some among the 750 ineligible applicants for option C eventually buy plots from original plot holders, then the argument for greater concentration comes into focus: the real client group's demand is more for C's small plot and relatively large building than for D's larger plot and no building at all. If it were possible in any way immediately to expand total investment simultaneously to reduce the degree of gradual construction by building more per plot and increase the number of plots, the argument would be persuasive. But with total investment less easily increased, a lower degree of gradual development means fewer total plots − satisfying a smaller proportion of the 2000 applicants for C and D plots. Less housing would result, and an even smaller percentage of low-income plots would remain in their intended use.

2.9 The current debate about standards

Another way to look at Arumbakkam is to compare its standards with those in Madras as a whole (Lakshmanan and Kumaresan 1981). Roughly 9 per cent of households live in public flats and tenements, with an equal proportion in private housing built similarly at or above the official norms. Densities of these neighbourhoods run between 5 and 50 households per hectare, compared with Arumbakkam's 84 and densities ranging between 100 and 600 in over four-fifths of the housing. Conversely, plot sizes in planned neighbourhoods prior to Arumbakkam ranged between 150 and 300 m^2, compared with the 40–220 m^2 range in the project and 12–20 m^2 most common in officially designated slums.

If 'standards' means the official norms, Arumbakkam clearly represents reduced standards. But if we take the term in its more general sense, the value of any variable descriptive of housing, Arumbakkam just as clearly represents increased standards. The families living in Arumbakkam enjoy standards far superior to the average in the city, especially when security, health and safety hazards, water and sewerage supply and other standards are added into the account. Given that initial investment per unit (Lakshmanan and Kumaresan 1981: 2, 16) was less than a sixth of the average in conventional projects, it seems almost certain that the project did more than a comparably costly conventional project could have done immediately to raise average standards.

The current debate about norms, however, gets stuck at this point. If lower norms bring an immediate increase in standards, might this have almost no positive effect on standards in the long run? If not, there is a case for retaining high norms, in effect trading immediate but temporary improvements for higher standards eventually.

Experience so far suggests that families in the fourth income decile and above, who occupy most sites and services plots to date, build houses fairly quickly and to high standards. From this group, sites and services generates extra savings for, and investment in, houses. Some of its members have assets they will sell and even accumulated savings, while others will endure a few years of exceptionally high savings. Lack of secure land and services, then, is the principal bottleneck, which large degrees of gradual construction and self-help can open. Drastically lowering certain norms, especially plot sizes and public reservations, which have a permanence not changed easily by successive increments of investment, would no doubt prejudice standards in the long run. Other norms, though, merely stand in the way of increasing housing production and standards. House size and building materials within six months of occupancy, initial infrastructure, quality of finishes, land use, and others that do not share the permanence of a public reservation either detract from families' willingness to invest or absorb public investment in core houses, construction loans, technical assistance and road surfacing, rather than in additional land.

For families in the fourth decile and above, the trade-off between densities and commuting costs makes large, peripherally located projects feasible in big cities. But this sort of project (Thailand 1980: 39), 'although contributing significantly to the improvement of the housing stock, will not be able to reach low-income households in a large enough number to make a real difference'.

Projects located on costly land would make a real difference. Clever site planning can extend the concept of gradual construction somewhat to ameliorate the pressures of land costs on long-run standards. Inside low-income neighbourhoods exists a variety of land uses besides housing. Small businesses, materials stores, markets and market gardens fall in this category. Over time, part of these disappear as, and if, residents' incomes increase, houses get built and families enter later stages in the family life cycle. Then, unlike initially, there may be demand for roads or open spaces that were before unfeasible except on cheap land. Given this context, a thread of market gardens let for rent would not add as much as unused road reserves and pavements to plot charges. It generates revenues for new projects while land development is still the essential priority; it also yields the costly land needed for roads in future. Several land uses offer similar possibilities for the gradual development of public reservations. Most, in the meantime, generate other income for public investment and possibly for families' direct investment in housing.

Yet, neither gradual construction nor self-help can fully eliminate the necessity for small plot sizes and public reservations, modest rather than high infrastructure standards and types of houses that families in the second and third income deciles have time and money to build. For this group, as for the ones above it, sites and services probably expands total investment in houses which, with the accompanying improvements in services and security, is not a negligible achievement. The land that government adds for low-income housing today, moreover, almost automatically ensures lower gross densities in all low-income neighbourhoods ten years from now. Over this period, densities are going to increase regardless of official norms for projects, and the prospect of moderating the increase for poorer families lies in more land rather than less land with large plots and public reservations.

There is a final reason why reductions in norms that go beyond the cuts required for gradual construction might eventually raise standards.

The 'poor quality' housing today's governments can develop inside sites and services occupied by low-income families should be easier to improve than any alternative housing these families will find outside. Tenure problems and site conditions in projects will not necessitate mass relocation. Secure tenure and good sites remove many of the serious problems of upgrading, and, with only moderately high densities, upgrading will become relatively simple. What holds for projects will, to a lesser extent, also be true for other low-income neighbourhoods, as long as sites and services has succeeded in slowing their growth. It must be stressed that these benefits accrue in direct relation to reductions in norms today: a small reduction frees too little public investment to add a significant area of well-located land to the low-income housing stock.

The possibility for effective use of price subsidies also increases over time under a regime of reduced norms. Governmental niggardliness and real financial incapacity now limit cash grants, input transfers, low-interest foreign loans and other forms of production subsidies to levels that cannot pay for much housing. Hence, many agencies try not to pass the full value of their subsidies on to residents, and instead to charge as if the subsidy had been less and use the resulting revenues to increase production in future. It is to be hoped that future governments will have funds from taxes and today's projects to increase price subsidies. Given then an easily identified, relatively simple house-building problem, one can trust future governments to raise house standards higher than they could if they had to deal with the same families living in worse houses in squatter neighbourhoods and slums built after 1980.

Should the scope for subsidizing high standards not increase, then high norms will lead sites and services to the same end as befell conventional housing programmes. Both will have been able to expand the supply of housing marginally, and neither will have improved housing conditions for low-income families.

Notes

1 The principal relations between final standards and self-help depend on the extent of family decision-making and on the income and subsidies received by the people in projects. It seems likely that middle-income groups will build houses at standards above the norms of conventional projects. But lower-income families in self-help projects probably cannot afford such standards and, while the families may build houses larger than dwellings in conventional projects, they generally will not have the means or the inclination to reach other norms. For a brief, comparative review of evidence about low-income families' housing and investment priorities see Burns and Grebler 1977: 220–4.

2 Throughout this essay, 'direct family investment' denotes the investments families decide on and pay for currently from their own savings plus unpaid family labour. 'Direct agency investment' denotes the costs of inputs financed by a housing agency. The distinction differs from the distinction between families' and governments' shares of total costs. The families' share comprises their direct investments and mortgage, hire-purchase, rent, service charge and tax payments. Governments' share is the subsidy, if any, on housing costs.

3 A useful review of sites and services projects does not yet exist. The World Bank perhaps has done most of the work to date on comparative evaluation, and some of this work is available in the form of seminar papers and comments in Bank pamphlets (World Bank 1978). Most of it, along with most information about Bank-sponsored plans for sites and services, however, is still locked up in 'documents for official use only'.

4 I have based the estimates on data in AFSC (1975) and interviews with architects, planners and economists who are familiar with Zambian building costs and had worked in Zambia in the early 1970s. Their estimates of the costs of using small contractors instead of family labour for the construction of Chawama's core houses ranged between 150 kwacha and 300 kwacha per house, depending on the amount of time allowed for collecting and separating soil to make blocks. (1 kwacha equalled approximately 1.4 US dollars at the official rate of exchange in the early 1970s.) The figures for costs of technical assistance are derived from the project's reported budget (AFSC 1975: appendix H) and a description of the nature of assistance, as contained in various sections of the AFSC report. The figure does not include costs of training the project's field teams, preliminary studies of soil conditions, and other items arranged through the Zambian government, universities and technical schools.

5 Data about families' investment expenses in sites and services are scarce. In the Chawama project, families reportedly spent about $200 of their own savings during construction, which lasted usually six to twenty months. Assuming an average period of twelve months and an average family income around $50 per month, families would have spent an amount equal to one-third of their incomes during construction. In a study not published yet, I found families in a Tanzanian project and relatively secure squatter neighbourhoods spending typically about one-and-a-half times their reported annual cash incomes to build houses over a period of two to four years, including a time before on-site works starts when families accumulate materials. See also Martin (1975: table 5.5), which gives some indicative figures for estimating saving ratios.

6 The minimum wage in the late 1970s was 480 shillings per month (officially, 8.75 shillings = $1.00 in 1978). Bus fares were one shilling per trip, and a worker commuting by bus from sites and services projects would take two or four trips per day, six days a week.

7 Plot sizes in African projects tend to be larger than plots in Asian and Latin American projects. With a few exceptions, African cities tend to be smaller, and still have a considerable agricultural component mixed into urban life, in the form of market gardens and cultivation for personal consumption on the residential plot.

8 Discussion of subsidy policies suffers from confusion about the meaning and measurement of subsidy rates. Invisible subsidies account for a large proportion of the total in housing projects. These subsidies, invisible in the sense of not being a specific entry in governmental expenditure accounts, include, among others, land grants and transfers of land at prices below cost, loans to agencies at low rates of interest, and uncounted interest costs during construction. The use of some invisible subsidies leads to budgeted construction expenses underrepresenting costs, and all lead to an even larger underrepresentation of total subsidy, unless such items as low interest rates are specifically evaluated. The most common measure of the rate of subsidy, cash grants divided by budgeted construction expenses, consequently gives a misleading impression. Because of this, projects planned 'to fully recover costs' usually involve large, planned subsidies which, when added to unplanned subsidies, keep subsidy rates in sites and services high – often above 50 per cent, I would guess.

References

AFSC (American Friends Service Committee) (1975) *Chawama Self-Help Housing Project, Kafue, Zambia*, Philadelphia.

Bamberger, M. (1979) 'Progressive development/self-help construction as a means to increase the low income housing stock', Ottawa, Canada, paper presented to and published in the report of the Sixth Annual Conference on Monitoring and Evaluation of Shelter Programs for the Urban Poor, sponsored by the International Development Research Center, World Bank.

Burns, L. S. and Grebler, L. (1977) *The Housing of Nations*, London, Macmillan.

Crooke, P. (1981) 'Low income housing in Malawi: an evaluation of British-aided programmes', London, Overseas Development Administration.

Foundation for Cooperative Housing International, Inc. (c. 1980) *Mansion in the Sky: A Lesson in Self-Help Housing from Gaborone*, Botswana, Washington DC.

Khan, A. R. and Mirza, M. I. (1981) 'Metroville I', paper presented to the Seminar on Sites and Services in Asia, held under the sponsorship of the National Housing Authority of Thailand in Bangkok, 5–16 January 1981.

Lakshmanan, A. and Kumaresan, S. (1981) 'Arumbakkam sites and services', paper presented to the Seminar on Sites and Services in Asia, held under the sponsorship of the National Housing Authority of Thailand in Bangkok, 5–16 January 1981.

Lazaro, A. S. and Lingan, A. (1981) 'Dasmarinas Bagong Bayan', paper presented to the Seminar on Sites and Services in Asia, held under the sponsorship of the National Housing Authority of Thailand in Bangkok, 5–16 January 1981.

Magembe, E. J. A. (1981) 'Sources of finance for individual housing in Dar es Salaam, Tanzania', Dar es Salaam, Centre for Housing Studies, mimeo.

Martin, R. J. (1975) *Self Help in Action*, Lusaka, Zambia, National Housing Authority.

Mghweno, J. M. and Satyanarayana, B. (1978) 'Objectives and outline of the first and second national sites and services project', Dar es Salaam, Institute of Finance Management.

Nathan, Robert R. and Associates, Inc. (1978) 'Preliminary report: shelter sector assessment for the Government of Malawi', Washington DC, United States Agency for International Development.

Robertson, J. T. (1978) 'The housing sector – perspective and prospects, Lusaka, Government of the Republic of Zambia', paper presented to the National Housing Conference on the subject of the Third National Development Plan.

Schilderman, Th. (1981) 'Labour for individual housing in Dar es Salaam', Dar es Salaam, Centre for Housing Studies, mimeo.

Seri Kirisiri, Prakit Tangharoen and Pramode Chaipoon (1981) 'Tung Song Hong', paper presented to the Seminar on Sites and Services in Asia, held under the sponsorship of the National Housing Authority of Thailand in Bangkok, 5–16 January 1981.

Somsak Nak Nguen Thong and Komson Suksumake (1981) 'Rangsit sites and services phase I', paper presented to the Seminar on Sites and Services in Asia, held under the sponsorship of the National Housing Authority of Thailand, Bangkok, 5–16 January 1981.

Thailand (1980), 'Present standards and prices on the housing market in Bangkok', National Housing Authority.

World Bank (1978) 'Sites and services and upgrading, a review of Bank-assisted projects', Washington DC, World Bank, Urban Projects Department.

3
Upgrading

R. J. MARTIN

3.1 Introduction

At the risk of being simplistic, this chapter starts with a brief statement of the advantages of upgrading, as found in the majority of situations.

1 It preserves existing economic systems and opportunities for those most in need, the urban poor.
2 It preserves a low-cost housing system, usually at advantageous locations, thus enabling the inhabitants to retain the maximum disposable income.
3 It preserves a community which has many internal linkages to safeguard the interests of the individual family and the group.
4 The alternative to upgrading is relocation in one form or another: this is socially disruptive and by usually being to a much less favourable location, results in higher transport costs and less access to informal employment opportunities.

Upgrading is not a new concept in itself. Haussman's boulevards in Paris could be called upgrading (from his perspective, at any rate) and most organically planned cities, of which London is a good example, have been upgraded progressively through the ages. Squatter and slum upgrading is a newer concept, though not as new as some may believe. The Dutch proposed an extensive programme of upgrading in the kampongs of Java as far back as 1938, and unpublicized schemes by engineers of good will, bringing modest improvements such as a few water taps, have long been a feature of many tropical cities.

Sadly enough, however, it has not always been the intrinsic merits of upgrading which have led to its adoption, but the failure of conventional housing policies to result in the production of a sufficient number of units annually, and at a sufficiently low cost. As a result of this failure an increasing number of people live in informal settlements, which are acting as the major housing resource in nearly all tropical cities. The government response to this has tended to be to treat this condition as an 'unacceptable', but fortunately 'passing' phenomenon. Thus it is assumed that the economic situation will improve and urbanization will be adequately contained so that the provision of conventional housing will once more catch up with demand. Anyone who has studied the situation carefully knows that this is an impossible dream, and that informal settlements are, without doubt, a permanent feature. However, no matter whether upgrading schemes are seen as permanent, or just stop-gap measures, they are being undertaken on an increasingly wide scale, and the 1970s saw an almost world-wide trend towards upgrading. The planners of 'temporary' upgrading schemes have yet to understand that their effect is, in practice, much more similar to the permanent ones than might be expected. Nevertheless the way that upgrading projects are formulated and implemented has been so varied and has generally been so limited in its objectives that there is, as yet, no broad-based body of experience that can be called upon. Because of this it may be useful to remind ourselves briefly of the difference between upgrading schemes and more conventional housing actions. We will then look at the objectives of, and special issues involved in, formulating projects before going into the body of the chapter which deals with methods of planning and implementing upgrading projects, and institutions and mechanisms for doing so.

3.2 The special nature of upgrading

1 Usually the residents control and have built their environment. If so, any activities by public authorities within it may be in conflict with the residents' desires.
2 In the case of squatters, the act of squatting is illegal and puts the residents in defiance of the state, and sometimes of private landowners as well. However, once the act of squatting has taken place the squatters usually, by being outside the law, have greater freedom than people in other housing situations (for example they pay no rent and face no external controls on land use or building). Upgrading, therefore, implies a loss of these freedoms, a cost that residents must weigh against the advantages to them of upgrading. A full understanding of all the costs and benefits of an upgrading scheme is therefore crucial for its success.
3 The participants in an upgrading scheme are not self-selecting, unlike

those who obtain a publicly owned house or a site and service plot. The only option most squatters are given is either to accept or reject a proposed upgrading scheme. If the community accepts, then each resident is in the scheme, no matter what his personal reaction may be.

3.3 The objectives of upgrading

Why is upgrading practised? This apparently simple question yields a wide variety of answers. Undoubtedly one reason is that it 'solves' the housing problem by transforming 'illegal' dwellings into 'legal' ones, thus improving the housing statistics. In the same way it also helps to defuse political agitation for improved housing by slum and squatter dwellers. These are general concepts that might loom large in political decision-making.

The detailed formulation of a project, however, can be guided by a variety of objectives, each of which has its own rationale. For example, upgrading may be seen primarily as a health project, either to reduce the risk of epidemics such as cholera, or to increase the level of public health so as to make the residents stronger, happier and more productive. Alternatively, upgrading can have primarily economic objectives, for example providing improved infrastructure together with loans and sites for small industries, vocational training for the youth and unemployed, and so on. Another objective is a social one, increasing the provision of schools, clinics, community centres, playgrounds, day care centres for young children and the like; and at the same time using community development methods to enhance self-reliance. A fourth approach is a legal one, which would typically include the provision of secure tenure, the progressive application of building controls and consequent extension of normal city services to the area. Finally, upgrading may be seen as primarily a housing process, in which the main emphasis is to upgrade the housing stock through a combination of house construction or improvement loans, technical assistance, secure tenure, the reduction of densities and so on.

The emphases in these projects are not exclusive, and most projects are likely to have components from more than one of the objectives cited above. But it is not only in the field of formulating objectives that important issues have to be faced: there are others which profoundly affect what can be and is done. The most important of these must be touched upon before proceeding to the main body of the chapter. They are: the problem of conflict and decision-making; the issue of land tenure; the question of appropriate standards; and the issue of the scale at which upgrading is practised.

3.4 Conflict and decision-making

The inherent complexity of most upgrading projects creates many potential points of conflict. One of the most important of these is the distribution of benefits and costs among the community: there may be tribal, religious or economic groupings within the settlement, with each group striving to obtain the maximum benefit for its members. The location of roads, for example, will have significant implications for anyone involved in commerce and industry. The location of schools and clinics will be of great importance to all, but some are undoubtedly going to benefit more than others. Likewise, since most upgrading projects involve demolition and resettlement, those affected by it may object strongly to paying the economic and social penalties involved while others are reaping only the rewards of the process.

As implementation proceeds, other interest groups may come into conflict. Different departments of government and/or the local authority may experience difficulty in co-operating as required for the smooth implementation of the scheme. Schools may be built but not staffed; street lights erected but the power required to run them not available; refuse bins provided but no means of emptying them agreed. While these problems occur in other projects, the complexity of upgrading makes it more likely they will occur, and the delays or changes in one component are very likely to affect the credibility and success of another.

Considerable potential for conflict also exists between the residents and the implementing agency, particularly during the construction phase, when environmental conditions have got worse rather than better due to the activities of the contractor, but also after the physical implementation of the project has been completed and the recovery of costs must begin.

These problems of conflict are greatly affected by the management system adopted, most importantly in respect of the relationship between the authorities and the residents, and the amount of power that the residents have to affect the design and implementation of the project. As noted above, this is the subject of later parts of the chapter, so will not be covered further here.

3.5 The key issues

3.5.1 THE NEED FOR LAND TENURE

It used to be a *sine qua non* of upgrading that land tenure would be essential if there was to be any improvement in housing conditions.

It was argued that the lack of security had a direct effect on the resident's willingness to invest in house construction and improvement and thereby led to generally poor conditions. As a corollary of the same argument, giving tenure could be expected to trigger off pent-up investment thereby generating a substantial and rapid improvement in housing standards. There is no doubt that this is true in situations of genuine insecurity, like, for example, some of the slums of Bangkok which are subject to periodic arson by landlords who wish to put the land to other uses, or the squatters of Nairobi, some of whom have resorted to putting up houses every evening and taking them down the next morning to prevent demolition. In such situations legalization and secure tenure will have the expected effect, but not necessarily as rapidly as was expected since there may be a lingering suspicion of the authorities' intentions. But poor housing conditions are not directly correlated with the lack of security. There are also the factors of poverty (the inability to invest anything at all in housing) and that of ownership (landlords not investing regularly in housing maintenance in order to maximize short-term gain, or looking for maximum returns from minimum investment, for example).

On the other hand, the granting of tenure may not be such an important factor because people often already perceive, rightly or wrongly, that they have tenure. Governments give recognition to squatters and slum dwellers in a variety of ways, and each one has its own significance. For example, numbering the houses can be a token of recognition. Similarly, giving trading licences, installing water taps, removing refuse, supplying social services and schooling are all signs to the people that there is an implicit recognition of their right to reside in that location. In these circumstances, where there is a high degree of *de facto*, but not *de jure*, security of tenure, it will probably make little difference to the rate of house improvement whether formal security is granted or not.

The importance of this is firstly that if the authorities are using the incentive of obtaining security as a way of raising money for the project, or as a way of inducing conformity with official housing standards, or as a tool in the recovery of costs (i.e. where the ultimate weapon is the withdrawal of the 'secure tenure' rights), then they may be in for a surprise. The bait is not nearly as attractive as it was expected to be by the project planners. Secondly, if the problems of giving security of tenure are insurmountable, due to complex land ownership patterns, requirements for highly accurate surveys of very complicated plots, and all the many minor technicalities that surround land registration and transfer, then the project planner need not suppose that the project will not succeed, as the very act of official upgrading projects taking place may be a sufficient indicator to the residents that they have security.

These are short-term views, but we should not overlook the long-term view. There can be little harm in pursuing the objective of low-cost tenure for all, as this acts as a legal tool with which the people can protect themselves against future changes of policy. It is not unknown for *de facto* security to prevail for many years, giving everybody the feeling that the settlement has a permanent place in the order of things. It is at just this moment that either policies change and squatters are re-designated as such, or that land is required for road projects, industrial sites, and so on. Fortunately examples of this happening are not as common as they used to be, since world opinion is beginning to be increasingly powerful in such matters. But if the residents did have formal security, at least they would be entitled to claim compensation, which would in itself be a substantial deterrent against demolishing their settlement.

3.5.2 STANDARDS

The issue of standards is closely linked with many others. High standards are always popular with politicians, who like to be proud of their achievements, and the higher the standards the prouder they are. But high standards imply high costs, which will mean the imposition of a heavy burden on the residents in terms of cost recovery or else to the authorities through high subsidies. In the former case upgrading becomes not a privilege or a benefit but an economic burden on the residents, and they can respond either by paying up and letting other expenditures in their household budget suffer, such as school fees and uniforms, health charges, food and clothing, or they may not pay, which will cost the authorities greatly in terms of lost revenue and staff expenses in trying to recover the money. Finally, residents may sell out to middle-income groups. While the last option may not seem unsatisfactory to the outsider (especially the politician) in that the standards will then continue to rise progressively, it nevertheless transfers the problem, in a more acute form, to another location. While the poor may enjoy the windfall benefit of this sale, in the long term the problem remains. This linkage with cost recovery and subsidies is an obvious one, but few project planners recognize that unless the residents accept the standards established in the project, they are being forced to consume a good they do not see the need for. This is discussed in more detail below, when we shall look at mechanisms for establishing standards in a project.

3.5.3 THE SCALE

Project scale is defined in two ways, both by the number of families that are to be served in one operation, and by the number of services that they are to receive. Experience in this field tentatively suggests that small projects are more successful than large ones, and that simple projects are more successful than complicated ones. Upgrading is such a complex process in itself that to try to do many things at the same time is confusion compounded. Let us therefore examine a little more deeply why it tends to become large scale and/or comprehensive.

Probably the most important reason for trying to undertake a comprehensive project is that, having waited so long in the position of being disadvantaged citizens, the people may feel they have the right, and quickly, to 'normal services'. To receive only one service at a time may be difficult for them to understand. Similarly, it appears to be simpler from the staffing point of view, particularly where participation is involved, if the staff can handle many facets at the same time when holding discussions with the residents. Residents will be bound to voice a wide range of needs and it is more satisfactory if there is action to deal with as many demands as possible. Thirdly, where physical matters are involved, it makes obvious sense to plan for all needs at the same time, as to deal with the matters piecemeal could be both confusing and physically unsatisfactory. Fourthly, squatter and slum upgrading policies tend to be approved rather abruptly. One day the official policy is resettlement and the next it is upgrading. If this is the case the problem is one of daunting magnitude. In nearly all cities in the developing world, between one-third and one-half of the population is living in informal settlements. Thus any agency given the task of upgrading will aim to do it as fast as possible, bearing in mind also that the city is probably growing far faster than the formal housing stock. Lastly, it must be noted that there are many linkages in upgrading projects. Health is affected not only by improved water supply and sanitation but refuse collection (which requires access), health education and curative facilities. Likewise the provision of services which increase the residents' cost of living may not be practical without also assistance in raising their incomes by such measures as the provision of loans and sites for small businesses, vocational training for school leavers and housewives, marketing and book-keeping training, the establishment of credit union and savings associations, and so on. Loans for house improvement may imply giving security of tenure which itself may imply some form of rebuilding to simplify plot demarcation, and may involve control to ensure that loan funds are incorporated in the house and standards are maintained, and the provision of a materials store so that loans are issued in kind rather than cash. It may also require that standards equivalent to those used elsewhere in the city are applied and therefore that some dedensification takes place. Thus upgrading projects have a propensity to become complex, which, besides the problem of scale, poses the problem of co-ordination, which will be discussed in more detail below.

What then are the problems with comprehensive and/or large-scale projects? Both types, by being large in terms of expenditure, also require a comparatively large staff to implement them. This may mean substantial recruiting and, if the concepts being applied are new, a variety of training programmes. It will probably require additional administrative facilities, vehicles and even staff housing. These measures characterized the World Bank aided projects in the 1970s, and while it is not disputed here that special cadres of people are often necessary and even desirable, the rapid formation of project units creates many problems which could be avoided by a more gradualist approach.

Another problem with large projects is that an enormous amount of money is spent before there has been time for any evaluation of whether it is being spent well. By the time this lesson has been learned, it is too late. By contrast the programme that starts as a trickle and grows gradually into a river accumulates ever-enhanced skills, acquired by the staff on the job, and can develop ever-improved working methods.

Comprehensive, or, as they are sometimes termed 'integrated' projects suffer from additional problems. The most important of these is that the complexities of co-ordination between different agencies and activities (already referred to above as a source of conflict) creates delay. Because one component is dependent on the completion of another there is a ripple effect: for example, the objection of one resident to being moved may delay the completion of a road; this in turn may delay the completion of a new water pipeline; this in turn may delay the completion of a clinic; this in turn may delay the beginning of a family planning service. If planned as discrete activities ways and means would have been found to avoid these interdependencies, by, for example, planning to supply the clinic from its own borehole. But once implementation has started it is very difficult to judge if and when the original plan should be varied, and even harder to put such variations into effect as they are bound to be more expensive. Thus although comprehensive plans are more cost effective on paper, they are often less efficient in practice.

Looked at from the perspective of the residents there is another argument against comprehensive projects. It is that by creating a big impact on the environment and ploughing large sums of money into the community over a short space of time they can be very disorientating to the residents. This type of high-speed high-cost assistance may thereafter come to be expected on a regular basis, and the residents may put their energy (hopelessly) into trying to obtain such aid in future instead of tackling the problem with their own resources, as far as they are able. By contrast, the item-by-item project spread over many years builds up trust and realistic expectations, and also helps to ensure that the residents' priority needs of the time are being addressed as and when the means exist.

The above arguments are not intended to imply that large-scale and/ or comprehensive projects should not be attempted. In some cities the magnitude of the problem is such that they must be both large scale and continuous. But we must be aware of the negative effects of trying to do too much at once, and it is an issue which should be considered very carefully at the earliest moment. If it is found that large-scale or comprehensive projects are required, then ideally the means should be found of making the scope of operations decentralized and localized so that some of the harmful effects of intensive implementation are reduced.

Having outlined, though very briefly, some of the complexities of upgrading and the issues raised thereby, it is proposed to examine in more detail the methodology for formulating and implementing upgrading projects.

3.6 Project preparation

There is a long-standing tradition of preparing projects in advance, complete in all their details. This is a perfectly proper and necessary procedure in the case of conventional construction projects, but it will be shown that to do so in upgrading projects is very damaging.

International agencies must shoulder some of the blame for this. Their procedures often require detailed specifications and cost estimates, and tight schedules which do not allow sufficient time for appropriate mechanisms to be established for formulating the project. Consultants, often foreign, are therefore brought in to study the designated project areas. The only tool they have at their command for determining the wishes of the residents is the traditional social survey – the one-way question-and-answer format. Meanwhile the respondent cannot even be told the full nature of the activity because at that stage no one can be sure that the project will go ahead.

Once the survey is completed, the project is designed, proceeds through the many stages of approvals, and implementation starts. There is no option now but to impose the package on the people who may still have no inkling of what is in store for them. Whether it is introduced in a take-it-or-leave-it style, or a more sophisticated package sold by community workers, the project planners have had the last word. By the time the people hear about it, it is too late to change. There has been no dialogue with the residents concerning the nature of the project, and more particularly no opportunity for them to decide whether the costs of the project represent good value for their money. To be more specific, there are inevitably a number of distortions caused by the procedure:

1 Project components and standards may not accord with the residents' priorities.
2 The total financial consequences of the project may not accord with residents' wishes or ability to pay.
3 The decision-making system for the implementation process is distorted by the fact that a top-down start has already been made. The implications of this will become clearer as other aspects are discussed below.

Let us now look at the first two points in more detail. The standards adopted in the project may be totally inappropriate and out of tune with the felt needs of the people. For example, what are the expenditure priorities within the individual, as opposed to the communal, sphere (for example, how much money should be devoted to individual house improvement and how much for water supply or sanitation)? Likewise, what percentage of the funds should be spent on roads, and what is the standard of these roads to be (low standard and great length, or high standard and short length)? How much should go into security lighting, garbage removal and the like? Similarly, in terms of public services what are residents' priorities in terms of education, health and communal activities. In the field of employment generation, should emphasis be given to large, low-cost markets, or high-cost workshops? If there are to be subsidies, how are they to be applied?

However idealistic such a list of options may be, and however difficult it might be in practice to hold a meaningful dialogue to settle such issues, it is nevertheless a necessary starting point. Without it project components may be rejected by residents and important gaps identified after it is too late to change. The experience of the Lusaka project may be used to illustrate the problem.[1]

The project formulation team had ascertained that the amount of garbage generated by the majority of households was very small, and therefore budgeted for shared dustbins. Fewer dustbins to collect would in turn improve the frequency of emptying. However, when the dustbins were distributed there was an instantaneous reaction from the residents: they refused to accept shared dustbins, insisting that they should have individual ones. All the dustbins were then returned to the council's local materials store in protest. Subsequently the Housing Project Unit (HPU)[2] agreed that much lower-quality individual bins could be used and the dispute was resolved, but not without other problems (for example, the dustmen complained about the number of bins to be emptied). Another example in Lusaka was the street lighting, which the residents considered much too weak. In the end the HPU agreed to substitute more powerful lamps, at considerable expense.

Such cautionary tales in themselves do no more than indicate short-term problems created by one-sided standard setting, and do not reveal longer-term problems. The most important of these is the question of cost recovery. If an appropriate solution is imposed from above residents feel, quite naturally, that they should not pay for it. If I go into a restaurant wanting a bowl of soup and, without being consulted, am given caviare instead, will I feel inclined to pay?

I would suggest that even if a traditional survey has been undertaken ('We are planning to upgrade this area . . . please tell us "What do you like about this place?" "What do you not like?", "What do you want improved?"' and so forth) the circumstances of the interview do not allow mature consideration of the issues. Even with more advanced questionnaire techniques (gaming and the like), the process remains theoretical as far as the respondent is concerned. Valid decisions will not be taken until three conditions are met: there is money to spend; the responsibility for spending it rests at least to some degree with the residents; and the residents have the time and opportunity to establish appropriate standards.

Such decisions cannot be taken by the residents alone. They must know the cost implications and the physically possible alternatives. Just as politicians rely on civil servants to enable them to make a judgement, so too should the residents be able to turn to professionals who can give them information to help them take a decision. The experts, let us stress, are required to support a decision, not to formulate it.

3.7 Implementation methodology

The implementation phase brings with it problems of a highly visible nature, such as the refusal of families to move, harassment of the contractor, and so on. The normal prescription for such problems is 'participation', but few agree what this means in practice. Moreover, even if an understanding of participation exists, procedural mechanisms for integrating the role of the people with that of the implementing agency, or even for solving disputes, are lacking. This section will examine these problems in more detail.

We have already noted the need for participation by the residents in the project preparation phase. Other decisions which must be taken are, for example, the location of new roads and/or walkways, water taps, schools, health centres and the like. Such decisions in turn have considerable consequences for the residents, some of whom will have to move to make way for the facilities provided. As envisaged here, participation implies that the residents have responsibility for taking at least the most important, and hopefully all, the decisions affecting the community.

The most important issue, and one of the operational problems facing the implementation agency, is how the residents will actually take the decisions. In many states – Tanzania, Zambia and Indonesia are examples[3] – there exists a party or quasi-governmental machinery at the local level which is genuinely accepted by the residents as being their leadership and mouthpiece. This therefore gives a starting point for participatory decision-making. Elsewhere, in Papua New Guinea for example, corporate decision-making systems did not exist in the squatter settlements prior to upgrading and the implementation team had to sponsor their formation (Shankland Cox Partners 1977: 173–180).

This is one aspect of the problem. The other is that there must also be a channel through which decisions taken in the field can be put into action. The constraints on achieving this are considerable. First, there are problems of co-ordination. The implementation team may have several arms, some of which are involved for only short periods of time, and at varying stages in the project implementation. These different actors present their roles separately, thus making effective response by the residents difficult, and causing confusion as to who does what. Sometimes different *ad hoc* committees are formed for each component, thus placing conflicting demands on the time and interests of the residents.

Secondly, staff with suitable skills may not be available to present the information and to discuss the issues involved with the residents. The lack of such staff may be due to cost constraints or ignorance about the need for them, but where, for example, technical staff without such experience attempt the role of participatory agents the results can be disastrous. Skills required for such a task are usually found in those people with community development training, and to a lesser extent social work training.

Thirdly, the staff themselves may have no suitable means of communicating with the executive levels of the hierarchy so that decisions can be acted upon. The hiatus between field staff and the means of implementation of decisions in the field can be very damaging to the credibility of the implementation agency, and also leads to a breakdown of trust and dialogue between the residents and the agency.

In order to make these issues clearer, I propose to take the procedures developed (but not perfected) by the Lusaka HPU and offer them for consideration as a *modus operandi*. The process of resident involvement in Lusaka started with the presentation of the project package to the residents, initially in large meetings, then in small groups. The next stage was to invite as many as possible elected leaders of the area (about 200) to a weekend conference, which had a twofold purpose. One was to explain the working of the HPU in detail, the time programmes for upgrading the settlement concerned, the role of the different arms of the unit, and to introduce the various members of staff who would be working on the project. The second was to enable the residents to decide upon the composition of a committee that would act in their name to take planning decisions affecting the community.[4] (An earlier attempt to have each section[5] participating fully in this process broke down, and all recognized that a smaller group was essential.) This was done, and the members duly elected. The resulting committee was named the Road Planning Group (RPG), and usually consisted of between forty and sixty members.

Once formed, the RPG had regular meetings with the project staff, usually weekly, though reducing to fortnightly sessions as project implementation progressed. They had wider functions than merely road planning, such as the location of schools (a subject of fierce controversy), markets, clinics and community centres. They also began to take an interest in overall project administration, and on occasion would even demand the sacking of members of staff for lack of co-operation or corruption, or otherwise demand enquiries into what they regarded as fishy practices. In other words, they saw their responsibility in terms of more than being just advisers. To the staff this was unnerving, especially for the younger ones who expected to rely on their superior education to bluff the people. But although such a relationship caused disturbances it was manifestly a healthy one of mutual respect.

The process by which the road routes were selected was very simple. Without any plans being prepared in advance, but after a general discussion between the RPG on the constraints in terms of budget availability and the need to distribute roads fairly among all parts of the area, the RPG took the project architect for a walk along the routes that it wanted to upgrade. Often several routes were examined and a decision taken on the spot as to which should be used. Such walks took place at the weekend, and after two or three weekends the roads for about 30,000 to 50,000 people would be planned in principle. The project architect and engineers would then put these proposals down on paper and check them for overall cost and possible engineering problems (such as marshy ground). One or two further meetings would then be held if problems had been identified, after which the agreed plan would be prepared and signed by the leader of the RPG.

The precise boundaries of the road reserve, and therefore the identity of the houses that would have to be removed, was left by mutual consent to HPU surveyors, who had no connection with anyone resident in the community, thus avoiding allegations of favouritism. Once they had done their work, the occupants of houses in each locality identified for resettlement would be visited and invited for a meeting of no more than twenty-five families. At this point anyone who objected to being moved was invited to do so, after hearing about the costs and processes involved. They could request that the detailed alignment of the road be altered (which was sometimes done, but not often), or more commonly the staff found willing movers who were living in nearby houses and would exchange their house with the people who did not want to move. Unwilling movers were nearly always the elderly or the unemployed. Only very rarely was the problem not solved at the local level and had to be referred back to the RPG – and no one had to be evicted by force.

Once agreement had been reached then the group of twenty-five was shown the resettlement site nearby, and invited to plan the area they were given (0.81 ha) in the way they wanted. Throughout the process, the same community development worker remained with the group of twenty-five, and even when they were resettled he was there to help them solve their day-to-day problems. His role at that stage could be likened to that of a courier of a package tour group, the man who helps to deal with the local regulations and bureaucracy, the troubleshooter to whom all can turn for advice. This then was the mechanism through which the residents took planning decisions. We now have to examine how such decisions were put into practice.

The main medium for this was the field team, a formalization of all staff members from all disciplines in the HPU, who were working in the field (as opposed to administrative and managerial staff at headquarters). The field team was led by any individual who had the necessary understanding of the process, usually a community development worker. He was not necessarily high in the hierarchy, and was often on a lower salary than many in the field team. But he chaired weekly meetings and ensured that all activities in the field were co-ordinated, had been fully discussed by the RPG or others where necessary, and he had powers, within limits, to direct operations in the field. For example, he could ensure that the surveyors concentrated on setting out resettlement plots before proceeding to an activity that was less crucial in the total operation; he could change the hours of work in the field to suit local needs – for example, instructing the materials store to stay open later when there was a particular rush – and had the right to suspend staff who were infringing disciplinary rules or otherwise causing trouble.

But such a role cannot be sustained without support from the top, and this support was given by the institution of weekly progress meetings, at which all senior staff of the HPU presented their reports. The field team leaders' reports (upgrading was taking place in several settlements at a time) could then identify particular problems and the necessary action could be taken. For example, if a shortage of certain materials at the stores was causing a delay in the resettlement programme, the chief of finance and procurement would be called upon to take special measures to solve the problem. If he could not do so, the director would be 'instructed' by the meeting to obtain special permission to vary standard rules for procurement, so that quicker means of obtaining the materials could be found. Likewise, if the residents complained that one of the staff was being rude to them they would do so to the field team leader, and he would raise the matter in the weekly meeting.

These weekly reviews differ from ordinary staff meetings in two respects. First, the meetings were the occasion for outspoken criticism for different professions and branches in the HPU, if it was felt that things were being badly affected by them. This criticism was painful, but also healthy: it led to a performance-orientated attitude to work. Second, they acted as a policy forum, and no new ideas or measures were introduced without first being discussed at length in these meetings. From there they would be discussed by the individual field teams if necessary. Thus the meeting took upon itself a collective managerial role. Where did this leave the director and his deputy? They now took on the appropriate role of looking at the longer-term objectives of the project on the one hand, and on the other, at the all-too-important niggles of day-to-day administration, reporting to the local council, the World Bank and the rest of the institutions upstairs.

The findings of the weekly meeting were distributed in minute form (about six pages per week) to all staff in the field, and a monthly newsletter gave staff a further chance to air their grievances in often blunt letters to the editor. If we were to analyse what made these meetings most successful, it would be the direct involvement of the community development staff: their training was to identify problems but not to solve them. In a most subtle way they helped the technically trained staff to understand the meaning of problem-solving from within rather than from above, and limit the power of individual officers, from the top down, to take decisions without discussion.

3.8 Institutions and mechanisms

One of the truisms concerning conventional sites and services schemes and upgrading is that they require simultaneous and integrated inputs

Plate 3.1 The process of resident involvement in Lusaka started with the presentation of the project package to the residents, initially in large meetings (as shown here), then in small groups.

Plate 3.2 The Road Planning Group, together with community development staff and technical advisers, walks along a potential route for a road in Lusaka.

68

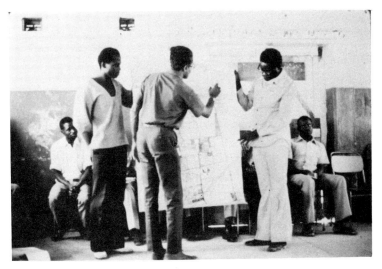

Plate 3.3 The Road Planning Group's proposals are put down on paper and discussed before a final commitment is made. Here they are shown being presented by the chief engineer, the architect and the chief community development officer.

Plate 3.4 One of the consequences of participation in decision-making. Residents demolished their own houses, almost for the fun of it. No one had to be evicted by force.

from a variety of different agencies. For example, in Lusaka's early sites and services schemes (1965–75), no fewer than five of the six departments of the town council were involved in their day-to-day operations. Upgrading brings with it the greater complication of participation and the legitimate demand by the residents that they should deal with a unified agency, not one divided into special divisions, each one of which is ignorant of and largely unable to influence the others.

Even where the degree of intervention by the state is comparatively low, there are few cases where the complexity of different inputs by different institutions does not work to the consistent disadvantage of the residents. The 'man in the street' drags himself from pillar to post in his efforts to get a house built. A multiplicity of Kafkaesque offices, forms, permissions and rules appear to be designed to catch him out. For him it is like climbing a mountain. Each ridge ahead of him appears to be the top, but when reached yet another ridge reveals itself. The rules of the game appear to be imposed purely to serve the interests of the bureaucracy and the ultimate achievement is not house-building (or whatever his objective is), but penetrating and mastering the bureaucratic system.

While the reader may have decided that this is rather an extreme view, overly critical of existing institutions, it must be pointed out that it is not the bureaucracy that is being labelled a bad thing *per se*, but that because the institutions were not usually established with the objective of supporting upgrading activities or even self-help housing, it is very difficult for them – or even impossible – to do the job without radical changes. It is quite unrealistic to expect a bull to run a china shop. A special approach is needed, and new institutions and mechanisms are essential.

This is not the first time that special pleas have been made for new institutions in the field of housing. The United Nations was active in the 1960s propagating the need for national housing authorities (NHAs) – agencies that would unite policy formulation and execution for low-income groups, without excessively close political control but still under the aegis of government. Unfortunately the record of these well-meaning institutions has not been good. The majority have come to specialize in the lucrative field of middle-income housing (usually labelled 'low cost') for which there is a steady demand and a respectable clientele. The distancing of the idea from the reality of NHAs or Corporations is probably due to the general failure of subsidized social housing. Their initial operational platform assumed that whatever they provided would be subsidized to the necessary extent by the government of the day. Therefore, without the hard constraint of affordability, and buttressed by a set of government-decreed minimum standards, they could do no wrong. When subsidies began to dry up, or be withdrawn, the basis for their work was removed, and their solutions had to become more conservative and 'economic'. Thus it is that with few exceptions NHAs leave self-help housing in its many forms alone, except to provide the design and construction resources for sites and services schemes.

This subject has been dwelt upon because the trends in this development are not inexplicable. National institutions with a brief for financial self-sufficiency are not well-adapted to the needs of self-help housing, which can be slow, complicated and unglamorous. There are alternatives. The obvious one is the local authority – the derided, plodding, ungainly dinosaur that is usually geared to keeping things going and little more. Integrated planning, in its widest sense, is a rarity, as local authorities are divided into departments which are largely self-contained, and none has the function of leadership. But for all their manifest failings the local authorities remain local, and thus subject to pressures from their citizens. If people have no houses or services, it is to the local authority that they turn. I therefore believe that if there is a way of creating, as it were, a 'local housing authority' within the local authority, this may work. But it will only work if it is integrated and largely self-contained, and is specifically disbarred from the provision of contractor-built houses. Its job would be to help low-income people to improve their residential environment and shelter. It would have the role of looking at the future growth of the city and making provision for that (by providing plots for newcomers, for example) as much as dealing with current problems of squatter upgrading, and so on.

There is another alternative with proven success in arguably the most bureaucratized nation in the world, India. It is the non-profit-making agency which runs the project from beginning to end, shouldering much of the burden of management but using some of the existing institutional mechanisms.[6] However, where it does the latter, it also typically assumes the role of helping the people to get the best possible service out of that institution. Where there is an existing, highly sticky bureaucratic structure such voluntary groups offer not only a way out of an otherwise impossible situation, but also a lesson to the bureaucracies of what can be achieved if systems were to change. On the other hand, some critics consider that their role is essentially 'one-off', which is successful because of the special energies and dedication that such a challenge raises, but which is not therefore a model for long-term involvement.

Hand-in-hand with the development of appropriate institutions must go the development of appropriate mechanisms for project control and implementation. I have already referred to the damaging effect of complex forms and procedures. Other examples are

– forms of land tenure which require impossibly complex surveying

and which therefore are never implemented due to a shortage of surveyors;
- payment collection systems which require people to walk miles and queue for hours during working days;
- building permits that require fully detailed plans;
- procedures that require instant adoption of new technologies.

These examples are obvious, and there are many others which are less obvious, but no matter how small the positive effect of any one of these, cumulatively they are of great importance. Creating new and integrated institutions will not of itself solve the problems either – a whole new way of thinking is required. All procedures must be considered carefully in the light of whether they are necessary at all, and if so whether there is any local precedent for them (I will give an example below). Thereafter, they should be discussed with the residents, and if necessary 'consumer tested'. Anyone who has had to complete an American income tax form knows what a disincentive a form can be. Likewise procedures must be seen as an important potential disincentive or bottleneck in the process. Such an obvious step as consumer testing is however a rarity as we all consider ourselves adept form-writers. But the needs of the bureaucracy cannot be overlooked either, and it is a foolish man who introduces procedures in the face of steadfast objection by the bureaucracy, as they will go no further. Thus there is an educational role to be acquired as well as a consumerist one.

3.9 Post-project effects

It is tempting but grossly simplistic to take a deterministic view of upgrading. In this view the well-formulated and implemented project would reveal itself in the spirit prevailing after the project had been 'completed' (that is to the extent of spending the cash initially set aside for it). We would see the streets, water taps and the like well maintained, probably with small groups of residents playing their part in repairing potholes in roads, cleaning out storm water drains, and so on; a glance at the records would show repayments of over 95 per cent in respect of loans and other charges; many of the houses would be under improvement while others would be being built anew; the local leadership would be organizing the construction of a new community centre by the residents, but with financial assistance from the local authority; a co-operative of informal sector workers would have just built new workshops and doubled its turnover; if there were any technical or financial problems that the people failed to solve through their regular meetings they would be referred to the local authority and a dialogue would ensue about the most effective solution. Such is one view. The reality is, sad to relate, too often the opposite − poor maintenance, no cost recovery system at all (by accident, not design), garbage lying in the streets, residents unsure about their tenure status, and their attitude one of distrust and despair.

These contrasts force us to look at the reasons for the familiar 'post-project blues', and to try to establish how important these superficially damaging phenomena are in the long term. The main reason for this is that the residents did not fully understand what was going to happen. This can happen with participatory decision-making systems as well as non-participatory ones. For example, when they were told of the proposal for new roads, residents could not picture exactly what it would look like (in just the same way, after the roads had been built, they could not remember exactly how it used to look) but yet they had an image. The components of this image would be vague but beautiful; the 'me' in the picture would also be carefree, better-off, and better regarded. No matter how we may fight these dreams they occur, and we place' more hope in them than we admit. The more inadequate the explanations in the beginning, the greater the come-down in the end. Some types of so-called participatory projects are the worst offenders in this respect. In their desire to convince the people that their proposals are a good thing, the planners and architects prepare beautiful drawings of scenes 'as they are now' and 'as they will be after'. The role of the drawings is specifi-cally to encourage people to react favourably, leading them to make the short-term sacrifices required by the upgrading process, in order to have access to the long-term gains. Such drawings in the Western World are used quite unscrupulously by developers to persuade planning authori-ties and the public that their development is not harmful. In upgrading schemes intentions may be more honourable but none the less harmful for that. But, however presented, the contrast between image and reality can be bitter.

This problem is caused largely by two factors − the separation of the role of the residents from that of the state, which causes this unreal expectation of a miraculous transformation through the magic of the 'state wand' (whereas in projects that the people plan and execute them-selves they have a relatively clear image of what will happen), and a failure of communication. Project planners must themselves guard against the growth of dreams in their thinking, and have particular responsibility to inform the staff who will be communicating the mess-age what will happen in precise terms. In most cases the only effective means of doing this is to show them, on the ground, using examples from other schemes as much as possible, what might be done. The staff whose job is to handle the discussions with residents will then be able to do the same, or bring in the designers if they feel that there are unclear points. Likewise, ideas coming from the residents themselves must be highly concretized by very specific discussions. If the idea of a new bus route is agreed, the residents may in fact be proposing a tree-lined boulevard, while the planning staff may see it as simply a 12 m road. If ideas are not clarified at the earliest possible moment – and it is always tempting to assume that both sides are talking about the same things so as to eliminate conflict – then there will be disappointment and even rejection when implementation is largely completed.

The second reason for unfulfilled expectations relates to the process by which the project has been implemented. Too often a socially cohesive and self-reliant community finds itself, its leaders and its rules transformed into powerless puppets, replaced by other rules and rulers. (The analogy with colonialism is a useful one here. Improvement is brought in at the expense of individual self-respect and to some extent freedom.) This leaves the residents feeling tricked into something they did not understand. Paradoxically, once more, it is the 'public relations' type of participation that is most damaging. In genuine participation this will not be a problem, and in the fully fledged, take-it-or-leave-it, top-down approach the residents will quite often feel stronger and more self-confident at the end, since the adversary relationship with the implementing agency will have brought them – the residents – more firmly together.

Against this background, let us look at the two commonest symptoms of the problem – cost recovery and maintenance. Both have a financial component: poor maintenance and the decline in the standard of services offered (such as water shortages or no refuse removal) will be a contributory factor in falling payments. Likewise, maintenance costs money, and without sufficient revenue it will suffer.

Cost recovery is a major subject in itself, and my task here is to do no more than identify relationships between it and other aspects of the upgrading process. The reader will be aware by now of the importance of stressing the cost recovery consequences of the project from the very first dialogue with the residents and throughout the implementation period. Many projects are, however, being implemented as if the subject were unimportant and only at the end does the government come round, like our aforementioned waiter, with the bill for caviare. When the people say 'we only wanted soup' the government replies 'too bad, you've got caviare'. But even when the message has been consistently presented there are often factors to be taken into account. There will be the genuine cases of hardship, and to penalize them mechanically will be to lose the sympathy of the good payers. Thus any penalties must be imposed with the tacit consent of the residents, who must understand the need for both cost recovery and penalties for those who refuse to pay. To make an example out of a wealthy businessman will therefore be acceptable; to do it to a blind man will not.

As mentioned above there must be a genuine desire by the authorities to keep to their side of the bargain and provide the services being paid for. It is possible to be over-optimistic on this score, and to assume that goodwill is enough; it is not. The majority of people will not pay unless they see the need to do so, and can get into the habit of doing so without a second thought. One of the problems in this connection is that to start to collect money in the scheme, while no one else in the city is paying, will also lead to conflict.

A way of making a positive connection between payment and development is to treat the initial investment in the area as a revolving fund. Thus any money that the residents pay back can be re-used for either communal purposes, individual house-building loans, and so forth. This has the effect of making the defaulter seem a selfish individual who is not playing his proper role in society, and social pressure can be brought to bear on him quite effectively, whereas in traditional schemes the defaulter can play heroic roles on occasion. Whatever the precise mechanisms to be adopted, however, it is clear that cost recovery mechanisms must be understood and supported by the residents. Payment must be strictly but fairly enforced, and must be seen to be reasonable in terms of goods delivered in exchange. In such situations the rewards of participation may be reaped. If the residents have actively played a role in deciding what services are to be provided, and therefore what they will have to pay for, they are more likely to be willing to pay, and to understand the need for doing so, than if they did not.

The problem with maintenance can also be eased by increasing the involvement of the residents. There is evidence to suggest that people would rather take responsibility for minor maintenance jobs than suffer the frustrations and delays of relying on the authorities to do it. If they do undertake maintenance tasks they should be charged correspondingly less for the services, and will have both the means and the motive to look after the environment well.

Such a move cannot be taken lightly and will depend to a considerable extent on the community being served. Even if it is accepted as being a desirable principle by all parties, there will be a need for some degree of training and formalized agreements on the demarcation of responsibility. Let me take an obvious example. Each shared tap is made the responsibility of one specific group of houses, and in turn the responsibility of one man to whom will be given a supply of washers, and possibly a spanner. He will be trained in how to change the washer, and how to diagnose other faults that might occur. The time and money spent organizing a simple tap repair by the local authority is thereby saved – a considerable saving if my experience is anything to go by. In one city I know, if there is a leaking tap, the resident has to report this to a housing officer in a local office. This man fills in a form and sends it to the head office. There another form is filled in which must be signed by no fewer than three chief officers. Once signed it is sent to the repairs department which sends a man to the central stores to get the washer. Another form is filled in. Then they, two men, go to the site and when they eventually find the tap and the stopcock they repair it. Total time: fourteen days minimum, two months normally. Actual repair time, including getting washer and transport: about three hours. Community-based maintenance is thus not only cheaper, it can be more efficient, and a serious effort must be made to find methods of implementing it on a wider scale.

3.10 Conclusions

This account of the problems of squatter upgrading has constantly referred to one theme – involvement by the residents, the people whose territory is being affected. It was stressed that the formulation of any upgrading project must come from below: this is both more effective and makes better use of resources. The implementation phase requires a genuine dialogue between the parties so that the people can plan what will happen for themselves, and understand fully the options that are open to them. In order for this to work effectively the bureaucracy must restructure itself both in terms of its institutional arrangements and the mechanisms it uses in the implementation process. Once these ingredients are met, the ship is set fair for subsequent success. But it was further stressed that after projects are 'completed', the participation and support of the people can have important effects on issues such as maintenance and cost recovery. These are all matters of operational performance and efficiency, which have been stressed in this chapter because participation is often labelled as slow and inefficient. But there are additional features of participation which it would be wrong not to mention, even if only very briefly.

I believe that participation has three distinct components. One is that it permits the free flow of information between the actors, and thereby ensures a product that better meets the needs of the users; this is what most of this chapter has been about. The second component is the psychological one: the person who has been involved in a decision finds it psychologically necessary to support it, even when things go wrong. Thus, during any project, and long afterwards when things do go wrong – which is invariably the case to a greater or lesser extent – the residents will react to such occurrences in a much more positive way. In a non-participatory project shortcomings in the project formulation, implementation or maintenance can be blown up into full-scale issues leading to damaging confrontations on subjects which could be solved quite simply if there were an atmosphere of mutual trust. In the participatory type of project those same problems will be accepted as faults to be solved. When the project implementation is over, the psychology of the relationship between the actors can also work to the great benefit of both in solving maintenance problems, and establishing a trusting relationship with regard to issues such as building control. The third component is that participation can act as a training experience, helping people to work together in ways that they did not before. Thus it strengthens social mechanisms and can give the people a political solidarity they did not previously have, as well as some of the tools to use it.

It may seem strange that it should be necessary to stress popular involvement so heavily, but it remains rare to find such an approach being taken. This is partly because implementation agencies do not understand the need for it in general terms, although this is improving more and more. But it is also due to the fact that professionals simply do not or cannot understand how to involve the people. They do not understand how to integrate the role of the professional, who has been trained in advanced techniques, who is fluent in terms of analysis, projections and calculations of all sorts, with that of the man in the street. With the best will in the world they do not know where to begin because they have forgotten for whom they are working. It is tragic that economists, architects, physical planners and the rest should now have become so accustomed to the idea of being servants of the state that they have lost touch with the concept of the state being the servant of the masses.

No matter what the nature of the government in power, upgrading gives an opportunity for the professional to get back to the reality of his role. At last he has genuine clients with genuine needs, and often desperate ones. He must tailor his services to those needs and priorities, and forget about many of the techniques he learnt which serve the needs of bureaucracies and fellow professionals. By involving the people from the start the planner then has the challenge of working with them to achieve a result of which all can be proud. As soon as he starts to see his role in that light, the confusion begins to vanish. The methodology of his work will begin to become clear. For an architect designing a private house there is no mystique about participation – for him there would be nothing so absurd as to design without reference to his client. Should there be so much difference between this process and the role of designers, and other professionals, in a squatter upgrading scheme? But that is precisely the problem. The imposition of externally defined goals on an existing community, no matter how laudable those goals may be, is one of the root causes of problems in the upgrading process. We are dealing with people's hard-earned niche in the harsh world of the urban poor, and their perception of their needs is the one factor that should establish their goal. This can be difficult for professionally trained people to accept, as they may find their perception of the problem quite different from that of the residents. They may feel that many mistakes are made in the process. But to allow a man to make his own decisions is the essence of the mutual trust characterizing a successful participation scheme. To force or trick him into taking a decision is good for no one. If there is one rule of success it may be this – mutual respect and equal rights.

Notes

1 The Lusaka Squatter Upgrading and Site and Service Project, 50 per cent funded by the World Bank, was begun in 1974. It aimed to upgrade four large squatter settlements with a total population of about 160,000, as well as to provide 4400 sites and services plots and supporting infrastructure.
2 The Housing Project Unit was the implementing agency for the project. It was established as a department of the Lusaka City Council (on a par with the others, such as the City Engineer's Department, or the City Treasurer's Department), but had a multi-disciplinary staff, including community development workers, architects, engineers, surveyors, technical assistants, accountants, etc.
3 In Tanzania there is the 'ten-cell' system under which every ten houses is over-seen by a local leader of the single party, the CCM (Chama Cha Mapinduzi, or 'Party of the Revolution'). In Zambia between twenty-five and fifty houses constitute a 'section' of the United National Independence Party (UNIP). In Indonesia urban settlements are divided into units of approximately fifty houses which form a Rukun Tetangga (Neighbourhood Association) with residents electing a leader from amongst themselves.
4 The problem inherent in any popular-based decision-making system is to ensure that it respects the interests of minority groups. Experience in Zambia showed that on occasion the planning was used as a means for settling old scores with enemies (for example, proposing a road that demolished houses belonging to members of the Jehovah's Witnesses sect, which was adamantly opposed to its members joining the party) and that some form of check to ensure fair decision-making is essential.
5 The party 'section' consists of between twenty-five and fifty houses, whether or not the occupants are members of the only permitted party, UNIP. Even before upgrading each house would be numbered on the basis of the section it

was in. Party members in each section elect their chairman and committees annually.
6 An example of such an agency is Kirtee Shah's Ahmedabad Study Action Group which has successfully handled participatory housing projects outside the bureaucracy, but for the bureaucracy (see Shah 1977).

References

Shah, K. (1977) 'Housing for the urban poor in Ahmedabad: an integrated urban development approach', *Social Action* (July–September), 335–52.
Shankland Cox Partnership (1977), *Third World Urban Housing*, Watford, Building Research Establishment.

4
Co-operatives in state housing programmes – an alternative for low-income groups?

I. GUHR

4.1 Introduction

The European housing co-operative movement has been a big success. Although on the decline, concepts and organizational forms are being transferred to developing countries where self-help housing strategies are being explored as a solution to the ever-growing housing needs of the urban poor. The provision of housing to marginal groups seems to have the same intention in both European and developing countries when low-income housing projects are started on a co-operative basis. However, the means to reach the same ends as in Europe apparently fail in developing countries.

The following pages discuss the consequences of 'adding' the concept of co-operative housing to public low-income housing projects in which building land and certain public services are provided and house production is left to the user – commonly called sites and services projects.

4.2 Failure in transferring European success and expertise in co-operative housing to developing countries

In Europe it has taken almost a century for housing co-operatives to reach the stage at which they are now. In the Federal Republic of Germany, leaving aside the Scandinavian countries with their highly developed and widespread co-operative housing networks, 9–10 million people are living in housing units owned by non-profit housing enterprises.

How all this was possible can be summarized in a few sentences. Besides a very prosperous development of the whole society after the war and the existence of a fast-growing building industry, the government gave large subsidies in the form of cheap capital and tax exemption. Non-profit-making organizations do not have to pay property, income or corporation tax. Furthermore, legal conditions were set to provide for the freezing and reinvestment of accruing revenues. Large funds accumulate as soon as a housing co-operative has repaid a construction loan, since its members continue their monthly payments as long as they occupy a housing unit owned by the co-operative. Reinvestment into more housing units is again supported by cheap capital. Thus German housing co-operatives have developed from participatory organizations into output-oriented housing producers.

Nowadays the idea of self-help in the sense of doing one's own construction has been almost forgotten. Today many members of housing co-operatives in Germany would only know the administrative personnel of their co-operative through whom they get their repairs done. This indicates that in most cases all maintenance is done by the co-operative and not by the individual member.

In order to face the growing overhead and maintenance costs, more and more small housing co-operatives are merging and pooling their resources. Acute housing shortages in Germany are over and the government has reduced its sponsorship of housing construction. These changes have brought back competition to the field of low-income housing. There are already private companies claiming to produce low-cost housing more economically than non-profit organizations.

The European success built up expectations in developing countries that housing co-operatives might be a means for implementing public sector programmes more easily. Housing co-operatives were seen as a synonym for organized self-help complementing, or even substituting, the organizational capacity of state housing agencies. Even with the assistance of foreign expertise in most cases they have failed. Unrepeatable over-subsidized prestige projects, or housing projects occupied by others than the low-income targets groups were the result.

4.3 State-sponsored housing projects shift from delivering finished housing units to the provision of building land and physical and social services

Before we consider the problems which housing co-operatives are facing in many public low-income housing programmes, a closer look at the inherent difficulties of such projects will help us understand the consequences of combining them with co-operative housing.

Let us follow through a hypothetical case of the procedures through which the beneficiary of a sites and services project has to go in order to obtain a house of his own within a planned settlement. It is assumed here that the participants of such projects cannot afford commercial housing, but are at least living on slightly more than subsistence income.[1]

At the moment when prospective participants are being mobilized, the project has in the main been planned, standards have been set and infrastructure works are already close to completion. Thus the most frequent and fundamental failure of many projects has already been made: designing the project not on the basis of users' priorities in housing and urban services, nor on the affordability concept, but instead on officially acceptable standards.

How does the process start for the user? After having learned through the mass media that there is a public housing project, the potential applicant will rush to the nearest place where he can get the details and conditions of the project. The officer in charge will only have time to hand out the application form for a plot. The applicant cannot complete it immediately since too many questions are to be answered. Later, the signature of a traditional or political local leader might substitute a thorough check of the answers given by the applicant. The completed applications are then submitted to the local administration from where they are sent to the central housing agency responsible for the project. After selection from amongst the eligible applications, these are returned as recommendations to the local authorities for final approval. This can take a long time. Hardly anywhere has delegation of power from central institutions to regional or district authorities been followed by successful co-ordination and co-operation between the centre and local authorities. Many projects suffer from the resulting delays in that successful applicants have left the place they were living in when applying or have changed their minds when a positive response to their application finally reaches them.

For those applicants still interested, the next steps are selecting one's building site, making the payments required and obtaining legal title to the land. In cases in which the central agency plans and executes the projects while the local authorities administer them, these three steps can be quite complicated. In the Tanzanian Sites and Services World Bank Project the successful applicant can first select his future plot at the district office (World Bank 1977: 24). If he wants to see it, he has to provide his own transport to the site. He will then receive a letter of offer listing all payments to be made in order to obtain legal title. For many this is the first time they learn of the actual financial obligations of joining such a project. Land rent and service charges have to be paid for the rest of the fiscal year. If joining the project during the fourth quarter of a year, payments also have to be made for the following year. In the first phase of the Tanzanian project an additional down payment had to be made covering 10 per cent of the assigned infrastructure costs which were to be repaid over twenty-five years at an interest rate of 9 per cent. The high interest rate was imposed by the World Bank in their fight against hidden subsidies. Together with stamp duties and other fees all these payments add up to a sum which is too high for many to afford. Therefore, again there are drop-outs. Only this time, by not making the payments but keeping the letter of offer they are affecting the project adversely, since plots allocated to them cannot be transferred to others. The district authorities do not have the administrative capacity to control this process. This lack of control has led in the Tanzanian case to the same plots being allocated to several persons, and to more than one plot being allocated to one person.

Those managing to make their payments and having received legal title to the land could now make a start on the construction of their house. Sites and services projects often end with the allocation of plots. When it comes to actual housing production allottees are left to fend for themselves under conditions which are forced upon them. Seldom are there projects in which the users are allowed to use a design which they can put into practice, the materials which they have at their disposal, control and speed of their construction and apply standards reflecting their present needs and potential. Conditions, restrictions and procedures in public projects make it difficult to organize and to manage house construction with one's own resources and consequently create the need for construction loans.

Financing institutions are relatively new in the business of providing credit to a low-income clientele in a field where returns of capital are spread over a long period and where control measures for securing regular repayments are highly ineffective. Terms of operation are totally unlike the lending practices in the informal sector[2] and are only gradually adapted to the credit needs of low-income groups.[3] Access to construction loans is therefore not easy.

To register a mortgage as security for a loan is seldom approved by a financing institution for non-salaried individuals. Evidence for regular income has to be shown in the form of pay-slips, a statement from an employer or by tax payment receipts. Extending credit to families drawing their means of support from the informal sector is therefore not possible. Again, during this process a number of potential project participants drop out. And again their plots cannot be transferred to others since the original allottees have already paid for the land. They might want to wait until they have saved enough to start house construction, which leaves invested public resources unutilized for a long time.

Those who are able to produce evidence of a regular income when applying for a loan might still have to face more obstacles before credit is extended to them. Let us draw again from the Tanzanian experience (Guhr 1980). When an applicant for a loan takes the plan of his future house to the Tanzania Housing Bank[4] he has normally spent the equivalent of one month's minimum salary in obtaining an acceptable plan. Cost estimates of his individual house then have to be prepared by the Bank, the duration of which will depend on the length of the queue he is joining. So he would have speeded up the process by having chosen one of the plans offered by the Bank, for which the cost estimates had been made earlier. If the cost estimates for his own house are higher than the loan for which he qualifies, the Bank will offer a smaller-type design within his income range. The smaller house does not allow subletting[5] so that the monthly payment for the loan and for service costs has to come entirely from his normal income. Subletting might have kept him in the project. Without this additional income, long-term repayment – even if other forms of consumption are drastically cut to a bare minimum – might be impossible, so that renting or selling the house and moving back where he came from might be his only alternative.

Attempts to lower costs by reducing house size and number of rooms thus have the side-effect of preventing the house owner from increasing his income through subletting. Reducing costs in a different way – through building material research then introducing research results to public low-income housing projects – has its own disadvantage in that it requires a considerable amount of manpower to communicate the new techniques or modified materials to the individual house-builder and to assist in construction works. And if technical assistance is not provided adequately the new proposals might turn into construction failures and thus even become more costly for the house-builder.[6] Similarly, convincing a financing institution to accept traditional materials seldom has the effect of cost reduction since in urban areas traditional materials are becoming increasingly scarce and expensive. However, this might make material procurement and construction organization easier for the house-builder because of his familarity with such materials. And in many cultures traditional house construction can be carried out by the entire family. But the extension of credit for houses built with traditional materials is rare, unless certain modifications in the traditional building techniques are made in order to allow the house to be recognized as a permanent structure; an example would be adding a foundation to a mud and pole house in East Africa. Such additional conditions again require manpower to introduce and ensure their correct applications which is hardly feasible for understaffed housing agencies undertaking such projects.

Looking at the process of public low-income housing production from the side of the user has shown us a variety of obstacles which are summarized in table 4.1 below.

Housing projects organized under different conditions might be hampered by many other similar problems which have not been listed here, such as construction failures brought about by the use of modern materials by self-trained craftsmen, or future maintenance of infrastructure which, if not properly organized, might affect the quality of the neighbourhood very adversely.

The conclusion which we can draw is that whereas in uncontrolled settlements a large number of residents manage to put up appropriate housing for themselves, within state-sponsored low-income housing projects the adaptability of house design, standards and costs to the builders' needs and capacity is ruled out by the very nature of such projects. Although the activities of the informal sector are increasingly being recognized as contributing to the housing stock in a manner which most effectively meets the demands of low-income groups, efforts to adapt public housing projects to the needs of users, and therefore to the characteristics of the informal sector, seem to be progressing only very slowly (see also the following case study in table 4.2 of a potential participant of a sites and services project who decided to build his house within a squatter area after the loan negotiations with the bank revealed to him the actual commitments to be made when joining the project and receiving a housing loan). The actual process of his house construction within an uncontrolled settlement is compared with the process he would have gone through when joining the state-sponsored project.

Self-help housing strategies imply participation by project beneficiaries. In fact, when housing production in sites and services projects is left to the user it is not just participation; instead the most difficult component of the housing process is left to him. When building a house within an unplanned settlement, acquiring land is relatively easy; what comes afterwards causes the real problems. Building within a sites and services project is therefore not easier for the individual since only the simple task of finding land is taken care of by the project. All responsibilities in planning, organizing and constructing the house are still there, however, and they are much more complicated than in a squatter area, as outlined earlier.

Popular participation has been identified in various resolutions of UN bodies as the 'dynamic incorporation of the people in the economic, social and political life of a country which would ensure that the beneficiary is an effective participant in collective decisions with regard to the common good' (United Nations 1976: 71). This has been interpreted by a Nepalese team of social scientists as

> People's involvement, as such, has to be understood in the following terms:
> 1 Participation in decision-making, such as in the identification of development priorities and planning of development programmes, projects and activities.
> 2 Participation in complementation of development programmes and projects.
> 3 Participation in sharing the benefits of development.
> 4 Participation in monitoring and evaluation of development projects.
> (Acharya and Ansari 1980: 251)

Table 4.1 Obstacles encountered by users in public low-income housing production.

Area of project management	Problems frequently encountered
1 Project planning	No thorough analysis of users' priorities in housing/urban services or of users' own resources[7]
	Due to the lack of users' participation in the early stage of project preparation, application of officially acceptable, but unaffordable standards
2 Publicity campaign	Information through mass media, one-way communication; no thorough learning process can take place
3 Application procedure	One-way communication; the applicant has to answer many questions not knowing why; again, no learning process takes place
4 Plot allocation	Delays through unco-ordinated procedures between centre and local administration; eligible applicants are lost
5 Payment procedures	Methods of revenue collection are not adapted to the payment capacity of project beneficiaries
6 Credit facilities	Rules of financial security and official mistrust result in systems similar to those designed to serve the financing of conventional standard housing and not of the type of housing being built incrementally in the informal sector
7 Technical assistance in house construction	Standards of house construction set by financing institutions and innovations introduced to this field indicate that the more control is applied the more technical assistance is required

Table 4.2 Case study: comparison between an actual housing production process within a squatter area and a hypothetical one within a sites and services project.

Year: 1975
Place: Dar es Salaam, Tanzania
Actor: Edward Akida
Age: 36
Family: wife
   five children of his own
   two children of relatives
Employment: house servant
Monthly income: 500 shillings (minimum salary was 380 shillings) equivalent to US $62 and US $47.5 respectively (1975 exchange rates).
He constructed his house within an unplanned area though he qualified for a plot and loan under the national sites and services programme.

Actual process: *squatter settlement*	*Hypothetical process:* *sites and services area*
Access to land	*Access to land*
Selecting of the site (informal network of contacts). Negotiations with owner: handshake; payment. Total time taken: two days.	Application at district office sent to headquarters. Qualification by points system; approval returned to district office. Formal plot allocation and letter of offer. Selection of plot from the plan and site visit. Payment at headquarters and request for preparation of certificate of title. Total time taken: four to twelve months.
Location of building site	*Location of building site*
Twenty minutes' walk to place of work.	1 15 km from city centre. 2 One hour's walk to place of work, or bus and twenty minutes' walk.
Cost of land (1 US $ = 8/=)	*Cost of land*
380 shillings (about one month's minimum salary).	10 per cent down payment for infrastructure costs, fees and land rent for three to fifteen months.

Table 4.2—*cont.*

Cost of land (1 US $ = 8/=)	*Cost of land*	
	Two areas of choice:	
	Area A	Area B
	806–996 shillings (more than two minimum salaries)	1200–1476 shillings (more than three minimum salaries)

Costs of construction	*Costs of construction*
Five rooms; mud and pole structure 6500 shillings (actual costs in 1975). (The same house with the same materials but with better standards was estimated by the Tanzanian Housing Bank, or THB, to cost 28,000 shillings in 1975.)	Three rooms; sand-cement blocks 23,000 shillings (as estimated by the THB in 1975).

Monthly expenses	*Monthly expenses*
50 shillings for thirty-three months as loan repayment to employer free of interest.	154 shillings for twenty years at 5 per cent rate of interest as repayment to the THB.

Source of Finance	*Source of Finance*
Own savings for payment of land.	Own savings and part of the reimbursement for the title to the land (806 shillings).
Reimbursement (1496 shillings) from National Provident Fund[8] for payment of materials/labour for wooden structure.	Balance of reimbursement for payment of type drawings, stamp duty, mortgage fee, valuation fee and building permit (815 shillings).
Loan from employer for payment of corrugated iron sheets for half of the roof, cement, external doors, two windows and labour (1640 shillings).	Loan instalments for materials and labour at the various stages of construction.
Loan negotiations with employer: time taken, one week. Moving into the half-completed house.	Loan application, proof of income, legal access to land, assessment of eligibility, selection of type design, internal approval procedure, payment of stamp duty and mortgage costs and release of first loan instalment. Time taken, four to twelve months.

Table 4.2—*cont.*

Source of Finance	*Source of Finance*
Renting out sewing machine and one month's saving by no longer paying rent to be used for completion of the next room. Four months' savings from renting out one room and no longer paying rent to be used for completion of last room. Completed before start of rains.	

House design	*House design*
Five room Swahili house with central corridor and pit latrine. No drawings required (no legal obligation applicable).	Three room house and pit latrine (THB type design). Drawings to be purchased from the Bank.

Materials	*Materials*
Foundation: none. *Floor:* mud. *Walls:* wood structure filled with mud, mud-cement plaster. *Roof:* corrugated iron sheets (gauge 30) on bush poles. *Ceiling:* none. *Doors:* locally made. *Windows:* locally made. *Pit latrine:* three oil drums, reed walls, no roof.	Sand-cement strip foundations with footings of sand-cement blocks. Back-fill and 5 cm cement. Sand-cement blocks and plaster. Corrugated iron sheets (gauge 26) on sawn timber. None. Timber frames and batten doors. Timber frames with wooden shutters. Block-lined pit, cement slab, block walls, corrugated iron sheets.

Supply of materials	*Supply of materials*
Bush poles, doors, windows, used drums from local merchant carried or pushed by cart. Corrugated iron sheets and cement from downtown shops or purchased from construction sites. Taxis for transportation.	All materials from downtown shops. Receipts required, hired transport.

Table 4.2—*cont.*

Labour organization	Labour organization
One carpenter and one helper for wooden structure. One man and wife/children filling mud into poles structure, internal plastering. One man for fixing corrugated iron sheets. Owner – organization and supervision.	Assumption: 1 from the economic constraints he would not give the entire project to one contractor; 2 from the attitude shown during actual construction he would hire different craftsmen and organize and supervise the project without working himself.

Facilities and services	Facilities and services
Access: two minutes' walk to main road. *Water:* two minutes' walk to public tap.	Two to ten minutes' walk to main road bus stop. Every fifty houses share public tap; possibility of paying for own. Connection or water connection to each house.
Electricity: no access, kerosene lamp.	Street lights, community facilities connected, and possibility of paying for own connection.
Waste disposal: pit latrine, hole for kitchen refuse. *Educational, health, religious and market facilities:* all existing within walking distance.	Pit latrine, public refuse collection, or public sewer. To be established later.

Summary of table

Actual process: squatter settlement	Hypothetical process: sites and services area
1 *Time needed to obtain building land before the project could be started* Two days.	Four–twelve months.
2 *Cost of land* One month's minimum salary.	More than two months' minimum salary.
3 *Choice of location* No restriction.	Restricted to two areas under development.

Table 4.2—*cont.*

Summary of table—cont.

Actual process: squatter settlement	*Hypothetical process:* sites and services area
4 *Procedure for obtaining finance* First using the funds available, i.e. savings plus loan from employer (one week's delay during the negotiations with employer). Moving in. Using funds whenever they are available for completion of projects.	First using the funds available for building land and loan approval (seven to eight months for bank to approve application), then regular disbursement of loan instalments until completion on the basis of site inspections by bank and city engineer. Moving in.
5 *Choice of materials and standards* No restriction	Following the bank's conditions and the official building regulations.
6 *Choice of labour force* No restriction.	Craftsmen with the ability to comply with the bank's conditions and extant building regulations.
7 *Construction costs* Equivalent to thirteen months' minimum salaries.	Equivalent to forty-six months' minimum salaries.
8 *Monthly obligation and duration* 50 shillings for less than three years.	154 shillings for twenty years.

The summary of table 4.2 shows convincingly enough why the choice of a future life within an uncontrolled settlement and of building the house in the informal sector was an easy one.

If we go along with this then we have to ask whether these are, and whether these can be, the views of those planners and administrators of public housing agencies responsible for self-help housing programmes. One view is that

Urban administrations, including housing departments, are staffed by lawyers, economists, accountants, engineers, architects, physical planners, administrators and so on, each with their professional abilities and their own particular responsibilities. The role expected of, and played by, each profession, hardly varies from city to city. Furthermore, these roles are generally little different from those played by public sector professionals and administrators thirty years ago

(Wakeley *et al.* 1976: 7)

These are the same people who earlier planned conventional public housing projects. There is little indication that they understand that the problems of this new type of project are not just bigger but that they have become fundamentally different. The change from an agency delivering ready-made products to an agency only supporting housing production requires changes in the organization of the agency, in project management, possibly in the urban tax system, new approaches to land use, changes in legislation, and so on, and, most important, it requires changes in the attitudes of the personnel involved. Success in such projects can only be expected with personnel who have the understanding that low-income project participants are not a uniform mass of house-builders, that they are driven by an immense variety of needs, and that responding to those differing needs is not feasible with the production of standard-type uniform housing, but rather by intervening only in those areas with which the house-builder cannot cope on his own, and by allowing every possible flexibility throughout the entire house production process. Such an understanding can only be obtained through learning during project planning and implementation in a process of close co-operation with and acceptance by those who are supposed to benefit from the project.

The following pages consider whether housing co-operatives, against this background, can serve as vehicles to channel state assistance to the urban poor and as a basis for participation and close co-operation between public housing agencies and a low-income clientele.

4.4 Common impediments to the promotion of co-operative housing in state-sponsored housing programmes

Recognizing that beyond the provision of building land and of physical and social services a great deal of technical assistance is needed by low-income house-builders in public housing projects, more and more housing agencies consider co-operative housing as a viable strategy for extending the assistance required to groups of project beneficiaries instead of dealing with them individually, which is almost impossible.

What expectations have been built up within a government agency of a developing country when drawing upon experiences of other countries where conditions are vastly different to those prevailing in its own? A. C. Lewin (1976: 304) summarizes the most common understanding of these expectations.

The main advantages of the co-operative form of organization for self-help housing by low-income households may include the following:

- Creation of integrated urban communities, not only for the purpose of providing housing, but also for the supply of various services and facilities and the promotion of employment opportunities, education and the raising of the standard of living in general.
- Internal control to prevent speculation and illegal transfer of houses.
- Collective system of financing and repayment by means of mutual responsibility which considerably reduces the danger of defaults.
- Gradual assumption of responsibilities for the administration and management of the co-operative by the members, and subsequently a considerable cost reduction.
- Mobilization of savings and self-help resources by the co-operative group.
- Collective maintenance and upkeep of houses and neighbourhoods.
- Accumulation of experience and continual improvement of operations.

In short, there is the common belief that shifting certain responsibilities to co-operative groups will greatly enhance and facilitate the work of the implementing agency of such projects. But comparing the major stages of the housing process, from the formation of a co-operative to moving into the completed housing unit, with the process through which individuals had to go will show us that most of the assumed advantages of housing co-operatives cannot be realized without making a number of additional provisions.

It is assumed in our hypothetical example that the 'Rochdale System',[9] which is the basis for the co-operative movement as it exists today, is understood by the agency. We further assume that the first experiments in promoting co-operative housing have already been made in the country so that the original Rochdale principles which were laid down for a consumer co-operative have been modified to meet the specific situation of housing co-operatives,[10] which implies that some basic form of co-operative housing legislation is already in existence.

The publicity campaign organized for the housing programme has brought together a large number of potential house-builders who stated in their applications that they were willing to join a housing co-operative in order to reach their common goal of obtaining decent housing. Have they already been brought together? If the campaign was intensive some might have submitted their applications as a group because they all work for the same company or government organization and want to form an employment-based housing co-operative. Other individuals might not yet have met each other. None of them, however, is aware of the extent of commitment which is required in forming a successful housing co-operative organization. When the housing agency has screened and returned the eligible applications to the local administration for final approval, there will be three separate piles of application forms: the first will be from those who have applied as a group; the second will be from those who applied individually but intend to join a group; and the third from those who want to build their house on their own. The last category will make their own way (or not) as sketched out earlier. The other two categories will require different treatment.

Guidance and assistance can be extended at the place of work to those who are all working for the same employer. Employment-based housing co-operatives may be particularly advantageous as their members know each other and the problems of selecting and organizing the self-help group can usually be solved more easily. In addition, they can obtain various facilities and services from the employer, including:

- long-term loans on favourable conditions;
- equipment, machinery and materials for land development and servicing as well as for house construction;
- specialized labour for construction and training of members in construction methods;
- centralized deduction of instalments from salaries and their transfer to the funding institution;
- loan and financial administration for the society;
- general organizational and administrative support;
- transport of members and material to the site of construction.

The employer may also agree to a few working hours being spent weekly at the construction site for as long as the construction work continues. The volume and character of support and assistance offered depend on the type of enterprise, its size and economic activities (Lewin 1976: 307–8).

With all these advantages, employment-based housing co-operatives still require considerable inputs by housing co-operative extension personnel for the formation and organization of the society and still require regular contacts with the project administration. The type of assistance which extension personnel can provide will be looked at later when tracing the organizational procedures followed by a group of individuals forming a housing co-operative society. The importance of regular contacts with project administration can be simply illustrated here with reference to the Tanzanian case, where six potential employment-based housing co-operatives under the national sites and services programme were all refused final approval for the acquisition of building land by the local administration. The allocation committee did so because it feared that applicants might be using housing co-operatives as an easy way of securing building land and thereafter planning their house construction individually. This fear resulted from poor communication between the project agency (here the Housing Development Division of the Ministry) and the local administration. The project agency failed to communicate to the allocation committee that it was to give preference in land allocation to prospective housing co-operatives under the condition that they prove their co-operative commitment within a certain period of time. If they did not, the right to the land might be withdrawn.

Leaving aside individualistic house-builders within our hypothetical sites and services programme, and assuming that the employment-based housing co-operatives are receiving sufficient support to become successful, we can now follow a group of individuals who have received the offer of building land to be used on a co-operative basis. If the land is to be registered in the individual names of the co-operative members, each of them only needs to make the payments required to receive the title to the land. Each of them is free to remain in the co-operative or leave it. This is the case of a 'limited objective' co-operative which can be dissolved whenever the members decide.[11] Prerequisites for registering the land in the name of the co-operative are the necessary payments, of course, and also a process through which the loose group of potential co-operative members is converted into a housing co-operative society, a legal entity which can be dealt with officially. Here co-operative extension workers enter the picture. Let it be assumed that the decision to incorporate housing co-operatives into our hypothetical sites and services programme was based on already existing experience of co-operatives in the country concerned, and, therefore, on the existence of some type of extension personnel. Most co-operative undertakings are started by producer and consumer co-operatives. Extension workers trained to assist such types of co-operatives are not necessarily able to work with housing co-operatives. Before a housing co-operative society is registered, intensive discussions have to take place not only about the advantages to the individual in joining a co-operative, but also on the subject of each member's future commitments in terms of regular payments for land, house construction and operation of the society, and self-help construction and other responsibilities within the group. The members need guidance and a thorough understanding of the process of housing production within a co-operative and of all administrative procedures designed for implementing the sites and services project. Instead of receiving assistance through the co-operative extension personnel, the implementing agency is now faced with the task of designing a work programme for the co-operative which considers all the possible problems which might arise, moulding this into an educational curriculum, organizing the training of extension personnel and establishing a system of feasibility studies for housing co-operative development plans.

In the hypothetical example we are following through, let it be assumed that the mobilization campaign was carried out when land development was close to completion. At the time the co-operative is formed the land might be ready for allocation. Is it now advisable to postpone further land allocation until all the above required preparations have been done or should other measures be taken to speed up the process? In the Tanzanian case, extension personnel had only been briefed, not trained, about housing co-operatives; a manual for the formation of housing co-operatives had simply been handed out to them without explanation and was therefore incomprehensible; and feasibility studies were made arbitrarily in the form of assumed income and expenditure estimates, since actual figures were not available. Co-operative registration certificates were then given as a basis for land registration in the name of the society. All this missed out the most crucial steps in the formation process of co-operatives. At such an early stage only a rather half-hearted commitment by the members can be expected which can only be improved by discussing in detail all future commitments and actions. In the absence of this, members would not be convinced that apart from initial entry fees and membership shares regular payments are already necessary at this stage to allow sufficient funds to be accumulated to cover all unavoidable costs, of which payments for land will be the first. A thorough learning process, guided by well-trained co-operative extension personnel, might help in collecting the socioeconomic data required of each member, in getting regular savings started early, in establishing administrative procedures for the society and in designing the details of actual housing production. Most important of all, it will result in members who understand the entire process and are therefore prepared for participation. It might also help some members to recognize at an early stage that they are in the wrong boat and should leave the group before more commitments have been made.

Finally, when the society is registered, the necessary payments for the land made and the legal title to it obtained, the question of financing housing production arises. Conditions set for public sector projects, as described earlier, and expectations of 'modern' housing types also created by such projects, do not allow low-income co-operative members to finance their houses from their own resources and at their own speed. The same financing institution will very likely have to cater for the individual house-builder as well as the housing co-operative. Eligibility requirements will be the first problem for the co-operative when applying for a loan. If the co-operative is formed by low-income earners, there will always be some who are very committed and can afford a loan, but are living on earnings from the informal sector. It should be possible for a financing institution to accept them since the mortgage on the land as security for the loan is the liability of the entire co-operative. It only needs the maximum percentage of members with informal income to be agreed upon. In any case decisions by the board of the institution will have to be taken and this always takes time.

Next come the issues of choosing a house type, its size and materials. Is there really a choice? For the sake of simplified administration, materials supply, construction supervision, technical assistance and equal rights for all members, all will have to accept the same house type. In cases in which a basic minimum standard house type, a core house or just a roof loan scheme is financed, a certain flexibility might be left for incremental development. However, these schemes often imply such a high monthly repayment that nothing is left from a member's income for incremental development. The size of the house will then be decided upon by the bank based on the assumed low repayment capacity of the user so that subletting as additional income is not possible. The choice of materials will be defined by their availability in large quantities on the market. The individual member is left with little choice but to accept the well-meant dictates of the bank.

When a co-operative has reached an agreement with the financing institution – which can often take more than a year – has made the required mortgage payments and has applied for and received its building permit, the next tasks it faces are planning the construction process, work organization and material procurement. While they might be manageable for individual house construction, the scale of housing co-operatives requires management skills and experience which are seldom available within the target group concerned. The creation of a housing co-operative service organization might be the solution. This could also take over on-the-job training of extension personnel, organizing all administrative procedures related to housing co-operatives, preparing models for feasibility studies, and so forth. As mentioned earlier, most agencies are newcomers to the field of low-income housing of a self-help nature and have to undergo a long learning process before they are able to cope with it successfully. During such a process of reorganization and rethinking, the establishment of a housing co-operative service organization will, in most cases, be beyond their capacity and they may, therefore, prefer to attack the problem with their own staff and resources instead of starting up a new service organization. Consequently, the services provided would have to be rather superficial because existing resources would be stretched thinly. For the members of housing co-operatives this means that they are largely working on their own and have to struggle for years to overcome the shortcomings of the public housing project. The following list of obstacles experienced by Tanzanian housing co-operatives illustrates such a situation. Figure 4.1 shows the agencies and personnel involved in co-operative promotion, the services to be provided by them and the bottlenecks encountered. The latter can be summarized as follows (they are numbered to correspond to the numerals in the figure).

1 *Half-hearted commitment by the housing agency, lack of co-ordination and lack of training by the office responsible for the promotion of co-operatives.*
The Prime Minister's Office, responsible for co-operative development, has had a long experience in promoting various types of co-operatives with the exception of those in the field of housing. Until 1974, guidelines, procedures and conditions defining how housing co-operatives could be set up were non-existent. Then a manual for the promotion of housing co-operatives in urban areas was prepared by the Ministry of Lands, Housing and Urban Development (Ardhi) in co-operation with the Prime Minister's Office (PMO). It was supposed to be introduced to District and Regional Ujamaa and Co-operative Development Officers (DUCDOs and RUCDOs) during their annual meeting. However, on this occasion the DUCDOs, who were to be the actual implementers, were excluded from the annual meeting. Therefore only the RUCDOs were briefed on the use of the manual and were to communicate its content and application to the DUCDOs in separate meetings. In those cases when this was actually

---

Figure 4.1 Agencies, personnel and obstacles in co-operative housing promotion in Tanzania.

Notes: (a) The Building Research Unit is a division of the Ministry of Lands, Housing and Urban Development. Its efforts have been largely concentrated on research into locally available materials and traditional building techniques.

(b) 'Ujamaa' is the ideological slogan used to define Tanzanian socialist development. It can be translated as meaning 'living together, working together and sharing the benefits of common efforts'.

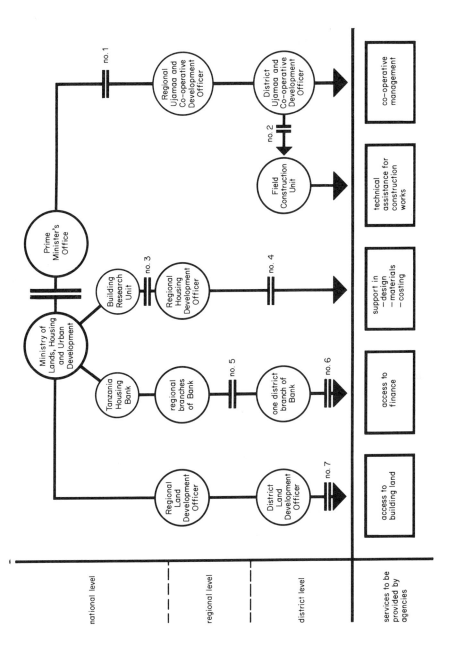

national level

regional level

district level

services to be provided by agencies

Prime Minister's Office

Ministry of Lands, Housing and Urban Development

Building Research Unit

Tanzania Housing Bank

Regional Ujamaa and Co-operative Development Officer

District Ujamaa and Co-operative Development Officer

Field Construction Unit

Regional Housing Development Officer

regional branches of Bank

one district branch of Bank

Regional Land Development Officer

District Land Development Officer

no. 1

no. 2

no. 3

no. 4

no. 5

no. 6

no. 7

co-operative management

technical assistance for construction works

support in
– design
– materials
– costing

access to finance

access to building land

done short-term training was still needed due to the complexity of the co-operative formation process. But lack of funds did not allow further training so that the DUCDOs, with very little understanding of the manual, had to start using it as best they could in the circumstances.

A similar lack of systematic action pervaded all spheres of housing co-operative promotion. In the Tanzanian case one can partly trace Ardhi's lack of commitment to an unhappy early experience with a pilot project located at Mwenge, Dar es Salaam. Other explanations can be found in the endless competition between the Ardhi ministry and the Prime Minister's Office in the field of co-operatives, and the absence of any clear division of responsibilities in this area.

2 *Technical assistance units hardly operating and absence of guidelines for technical assistance.*

The existing Rural Field Construction Units (FCUs) assisting village development projects were also supposed to be established in urban areas to assist housing co-operatives. Due to shortfalls in manpower, equipment and vehicles, the existing FCUs cannot be considered as operating fully in more than a few rural districts, so that the extension of their working field to urban areas is still to come. Also in which way they might assist housing co-operatives has still to be defined.

3 *Research results in building materials not reaching low-income house-builders.*

A considerable amount of research has been undertaken by the Building Research Unit (BRU) to support low-income housing production. Only a few attempts have been made to make the findings available to low-income house-builders. The first isolated practical approach, the production of photo posters with a few Kiswahili subtitles, has since faded away.

4 *Promotion personnel for housing development almost non-existent.*

Regional Housing Development Officers were only sent to the regions in 1979 so their impact in supporting low-income housing production is yet to be seen. Furthermore, guidelines for their assistance to housing co-operatives are non-existent.

5 *The financing institution concerned is only gradually developing procedures for housing co-operatives.*

The Tanzania Housing Bank (THB) as successor to the Permanent Housing Finance Company has had to find its own way in assisting low-income housing. Type designs suitable for low-income earners, procedures for cost estimates, eligibility requirements, are all still being gradually developed so that the operations of the THB cannot yet be seen in the low-income housing field.

Due to the problems experienced in financing the first housing co-operatives, which were established at a time when expertise on housing co-operative promotion was totally lacking, a certain reluctance to assist more housing co-operatives is understandable, especially when no firm commitment can be detected from the side of the two ministries concerned.

6 *Remoteness of the financing institution.*
The approach of bringing services to the people has only just started by the opening of one district office of the THB in one of the squatter improvement areas in Dar es Salaam.

7 *Lack of co-ordination affecting access to building land.*
Co-ordination of assistance to housing co-operatives is totally lacking, probably one of the results of low-level commitment by the government to housing co-operative promotion. This situation also affects the provision of building land for co-operatives, as mentioned earlier.

The Tanzanian efforts in low-income housing are not a special case. There are other countries where similarly unsuccessful attempts have been made. This experience shows that low-income self-help housing programmes as presently implemented in many countries are not very conducive to self-help efforts by low-income earners. Adding another problem child of self-help housing strategies like housing co-operative promotion does not necessarily facilitate the struggle for housing for those who need it most.

Are there any other solutions? There will be many in many different contexts. All of them will depend on the willingness to create conditions compatible with the capacity and resources of low-income housebuilders. In the following section an attempt is made to outline some of the prerequisites for a more adequate support for low-income housing production.

4.5 Conclusions

We are now left with the question whether public sector self-help housing programmes can be made compatible with the capacity and resources of low-income house-builders, and, if so, what role can housing co-operatives play? The answer to the first question is certainly 'yes'. The solutions do not lie in the rearrangement of already proven technology, procedures, and so on, nor in a high degree of institutional change. These have to come later. Effective support for low-income housing production will only be possible through the urban government being sufficiently politically flexible to accept that

- beyond a certain size of organization, centralized housing supply systems become counter-productive, and that
- low-income house-builders know best how to create housing solutions corresponding to their variety of demands.

With this understanding, public sector self-help housing programmes can still be seen as the supplier of building land and urban services, but designed however with standards based on affordability by the target group and therefore requiring the lowest possible regular payments. If we agree that central planning should be the complement of local control, then all restrictions, regulations, by-laws, etc. presently applied which prevent local control from becoming effective should be discarded, so that low-income house-builders can in public sector projects embark upon housing production on similar conditions to those prevailing in unplanned settlements. There they can use a house design familiar to them, with house size reflecting their present needs and can use the materials which are at their disposal at their own speed.

The answer to the second question – what role housing co-operatives can play – will have to be a general one since implementation conditions will differ in all projects. However, on the basis of the provisions given in the previous paragraphs, it can be said that co-operative service organizations could then act as mediators between housing agency and project beneficiaries and assist low-income house-builders more in reaching the basis for starting housing production than in the actual construction process. This could be organized in the form of services provided to project beneficiaries as well as to the housing agency in various fields, such as:

- organizing potential project participants into co-operatives;
- providing information on project outline, financial obligations and technical details;
- identifying user priorities in different project components;
- providing feedback to the housing agency;
- assisting in payment procedures;
- offering technical advice on construction materials and the use of building land only to those individuals who request it;
- organizing maintenance of public facilities.

In all those cases in which the state is willing to subsidize those groups who would not otherwise have access to formal sector housing, following the above proposals would allow for the provision of subsidies in the form of service organizations. These are in a position to channel scarce public resources through housing co-operatives to a much larger group of beneficiaries, and much more effectively, than is presently the case in most public sector low-income housing projects.

Notes

1 Here I follow Turner (1976: 54) in seeing subsistence income as the income of which a person, family or household must spend between 80 and 90 per cent on food and fuel alone if they are to eat well enough to keep themselves in good health.

2 Activities in the informal sector according to ILO criteria can be described as including the following characteristics:

  – ease of entry
  – reliance on indigenous resources
  – small scale of operations
  – labour-intensive technology
  – skills acquired outside the formal systems
  – unregulated and competitive markets
  – family ownership of enterprise   (ILO 1973: 6)

3 Such formal sector institutions as referred to here require of applicants a safe guarantee for the loan requested, high income, regular repayments and provide disbursement in predetermined stages. This contrasts with informal sector practices whereby the money is handed over on request and the most commonly applied condition for a loan is that the lender knows his client.

4 The Tanzania Housing Bank was established at the start of the National Sites and Services Programme and is the successor of the Permanent Housing Finance Company, an institution which had been financing middle- and high-income housing.

5 A survey made in 1974 within an unauthorized settlement in Dar es Salaam revealed that 95 per cent of the 151 members of a housing co-operative interviewed planned to build a six room house and 90 per cent planned to sublet an average of three rooms (Tanzania 1974).

6 This is to say that since the development of new techniques is much easier than creating the conditions for their adoption, technical advisers should refrain from overburdening low-income house-builders with their new inventions; instead, they should limit themselves to advising on how to avoid or correct construction mistakes made by their clients.

7 I am referring here to the planning approach of public housing projects and not to the technical aspects of project planning. For the latter sufficient experience has been accumulated during the 1970s to avoid those technical planning mistakes which characterized the beginnings of sites and services projects. In Bertaud et al. (1978), for example, a model for project planning is developed which is based upon affordability rather than the arbitrarily defined minimum standards applied in early projects.

8 All civil servants and employees of companies employing ten or more persons automatically become members of the National Provident Fund,

thus qualifying for an old-age pension, the rights to which can be bought out on leaving the job.

9 On 21 December 1844, twenty-eight poor mill workers founded the 'Rochdale Society of Equitable Pioneers', opened a co-operative shop and laid down guidelines for their co-operative venture which, as the seven 'Rochdale principles', have influenced co-operative efforts all over the world:

   i Open membership to all who will co-operate in good faith; without restriction as to race, colour or creed.

   ii Each member shall have one vote and only one vote and there shall be no proxy voting.

   iii Capital shall receive a limited and predetermined rate of interest.

   iv Net savings shall be distributed to members on the basis of their patronage of the association's goods and services.

   v All trading shall be done on a cash basis at fair market rates.

   vi Accounts shall be audited regularly and reports made so that members may discuss the association's affairs intelligently and act accordingly.

   vii Frequent discussion meetings shall be held by the members in order to consider the current state and possible development of their association.
(Dodge 1971: 1)

10 The principles and procedures which are most often applied to housing co-operatives consist essentially of the original seven but may also include such practical guidelines as:

   i The establishment of adequate reserves to protect the operation and equity of members.

   ii The option of co-operatives to repurchase homes of retiring members to eliminate speculation.

   iii The provision of adequate community facilities and the encouragement of community activities and undertakings.   (Dodge 1971: 1)

11 Limited objective housing co-operatives might be established for one or more of the following objectives:

- acquiring and subdividing land
- arranging the infrastructure required like roads, water and electricity supply
- project planning and design
- purchase and transport of building materials
- house construction
- gaining access to finance
- maintenance of buildings
- community facilities

As soon as any of these objectives is achieved, or when the mortgage loans have been redeemed, the co-operative has fulfilled its purpose and is dissolved.

References

Acharya, R. and Ansari, H. (1980) *Basic Needs and Governmental Services. An Area Study of Bhaktapur Town Panchayat, Nepal*, Kathmandu, Tribhuvan University, Centre for Economic Development and Administration.

Bertaud, A., Bertaud, M. and Wright, J. (1978) *A Model for Analyzing Alternatives in Urban Project Design*, Washington DC, CITRUD.

Dodge, R. (1971) *Cooperative Housing. Ideas and Methods Exchange No. 52*, Washington DC, Agency for International Development, Office of International Affairs, Department of Housing and Urban Development.

Guhr, I. (1980) 'Cooperative housing in urban Tanzania', *Habitat International*, (4), 355–62.

ILO (1973) *Employment, Incomes and Equality: A Strategy for Increasing Productive Employment in Kenya*, Geneva, International Labour Office.

Lewin, A. C. (1976) *Self-Help Housing through Co-operatives*, Cologne, published by author.

Tanzania (1974) *Survey of Mwito Housing Cooperative Society Ltd*, Dar es Salaam, Ministry of Lands, Housing and Urban Development, Housing Development Division.

Turner, J. (1976) *Housing by People*, London, Marion Boyars.

United Nations (1976) *Report of Habitat: United Nations Conference on Human Settlements*, New York, United Nations.

Wakely, P., Schmetzer, H. and Mumtaz, B. (1976) *Urban Housing Strategies. Education and Realization*, London, Pitman.

World Bank (1977) *Tanzania: The Second National Sites and Services Project*, Washington DC, World Bank, Urban Projects Department.

5
From building to enabling housing strategies in Asia: institutional problems

E. WEGELIN

5.1 Introduction

Resolving the needs of low-income groups for shelter will not be an easy task. The problems, essentially institutional, are rooted in long-entrenched traditions, prejudices and practices, and to overcome them will require a sustained effort. Reform will be hastened, however, by the changes that are taking place rapidly in the cities themselves, producing both stresses and strains in the social fabric and a growing willingness to experiment with new solutions.

(Churchill *et al.* 1980: 10)

This quote may seem to be a platitude, but it takes on additional meaning when related to the problems surrounding sites and services and upgrading. Such programmes, here called 'enabling strategies', are increasingly being adopted in the Third World. Experience with their implementation is beginning to demonstrate that financially as well as technically they can be effective in solving urban low-income housing problems. In contrast to earlier approaches of private sector housing combined with state provision of complete housing for the poor, sites and services and upgrading by and large can cater to the effective demand of low-income groups. Their large-scale implementation is not necessarily hampered by the serious affordability problems that make complete housing unfeasible. Unsustainably large levels of subsidy are not required to bring sites and services within reach of poor families. The families can and will save towards and invest in housing tailored to their demand.

The low-income housing problem in Third World cities is essentially a supply problem. The failure of the overall supply system raises housing prices and thus cuts off part of the effective demand for housing. Why does the supply system fail? Not because it is technically impossible to supply housing to the cut-off section of effective housing demand. Techniques are available to build cheap and secure housing with satisfactory sanitary infrastructure at standards the poor can afford. This is clearly demonstrated in squatter areas, slum areas, 'pirate' housing development and other non-official segments of the supply system in major cities in Third World countries.[1] The problem is that such housing development is often not considered as contributing positively to housing supply and is therefore suppressed rather than supported by government intervention. This impedes the growth of overall supply and contributes to high prices. Such counter-productive policies result from institutional and attitudinal bottlenecks. Yet, against the background of rapid urbanization, policy-makers have little choice in the long run. The official marginalization of a substantial part of the population will not improve housing, and ultimately it will lead to bitter confrontation and destabilization of governments. In the short run, however, problems of vested interests, static bureaucracies, class and educational prejudices hamper the implementation of technically effective solutions that enable low-income families to invest in housing.

This chapter documents some of these problems in the implementation of self-help housing strategies in Asia. The first of the following sections discusses a number of elements essential for enabling strategies to work, such as the provision of land and infrastructure, attitudes toward self-help construction, employment programmes, finance and organization. The subsequent sections discuss common institutional bottlenecks in areas of policy formulation, planning, implementation and estate management. This is followed by a discussion of the role of outside donor organizations, after which an attempt is made to pull the strands together to identify common causes of institutional bottlenecks. Finally, institutional problems are looked at in a dynamic sense: are things getting better or worse?

5.2 Essential elements

5.2.1 LAND

Availability of adequate and suitable land is of paramount importance to the success of enabling housing strategies. According to a recent World Bank projection of world poverty (Churchill *et al.* 1980: 3), the absolute number of the rural poor is expected to decline significantly in the period 1980–2000 (from 79 million to 56 million households) whereas the number of the urban poor is likely to grow from the present 41 million to 74 million households. While these figures cannot indicate more than an order of magnitude, they illustrate that staggering numbers are involved. In Asia and the Pacific alone, according to this projection, the number of poor households in urban areas will increase by 20.2 million during the twenty-year period. All these households will need land for housing. By the year 2000, they will have obtained that: they will be housed somewhere, somehow. Urban land policies in the years to come will largely determine if they will be efficiently and harmoniously integrated in the urban social fabric, or if they will be marginalized and alienated at the risk of violent confrontation with the established urban élite.

A similar remark applies to the urban poor today: no doubt they are housed (at least the overwhelming majority, except street sleepers), but often at unreasonably and unnecessarily low standards.

Urban land suitable to make enabling strategies work must come with security of tenure sufficient to unleash the potential of the poor to build and invest in their houses. Security might take any of several legal forms, but the minimum sufficient security must contain safeguards against expropriation and demolition. One can see in slums in Bangkok that in spite of the fact that building a house in wood is now more expensive than building in brick or block and cement, people continue building in wood unless sufficient security of tenure is provided. The reason is not difficult to find: in case of eviction, a wooden house is easily dismantled and can be salvaged to a larger extent than a cement, brick and mortar structure.

Urban land for the poor must be in the right location, close to employment. Where a choice exists between cheap land and high commuting costs, on the one hand, or expensive land and low commuting costs, on the other hand, the first alternative does not necessarily make housing more affordable.

Land must be made available in large quantity. It is not only the poor who need land. If insufficient land is made available, it will, sooner or later, be snapped up by the not-so-poor. Competition for land will always remain in a situation of rapid urban population growth and finite land supply. This will tend to increase urban land prices over time even under the most favourable circumstances. The effect of this for the poor must be cushioned by land policies which maximize supply of plots and take advantage of the definite sub-markets for urban land in which different groups of buyers and sellers operate. Land acquisition and particularly land development (control) policies should be oriented towards making land in the market attractive to the poor and relatively unattractive to the not-so-poor. Land use and plot size standards, infrastructure standards and lease, rent and sale conditions can be used as instruments in achieving this.

In short, for enabling strategies to succeed, land must be secure, suitably located, and in sufficient supply. This places specific requirements on land acquisition and disposal policies, as well as land development standards, which will be discussed later in this chapter.

5.2.2 INFRASTRUCTURE

For enabling strategies to improve housing conditions, a minimum of infrastructure must be provided. On land alone, people can build houses, but the environment would remain substandard without public water supply, drainage, sewage disposal, solid waste disposal, etc. This also applies to access to social services, medical services, education and community development. Inadequacy of such services leads to serious inefficiencies.

Paradoxically, inadequate services are often caused by the unrealistically high, prescribed standards of infrastructure. It is largely a matter of distributing the available resources: a little bit for everybody or much for some and nothing to the remainder. An unbalanced distribution results in high costs for the deprived group (e.g. to buy water from water vendors, to go to distant schools or clinics), serious health problems and frustration of further improvements in houses. In over-provided areas, it results in high costs and waste (under-utilized roads, unworkable sewerage systems).

Lopsided distribution of infrastructure usually goes hand in hand with substantial overall shortages of infrastructure and services and unrealistically low service charges. Governments are unable sufficiently to extend provision of infrastructure services partly because of implementation capacity problems (lack of sufficiently trained staff, organizational deficiencies), partly because of acute shortages of money and partly because of years of deliberate neglect, when it was felt that slums and squatter areas would sooner or later be cleared anyway.

Major roads, water and sewer lines, drainage channels, garbage disposal, and educational and medical services will have to be handled largely by governmental organizations. It is only at the receiving end of the infrastructure distribution system that residents can contribute significantly (e.g. in the provision of minor roads and drains, in garbage collection to a central collection point where municipal services take over). It is therefore essential that governments provide an adequate infrastructural network within which residents and community action can function. In order to do this efficiently, standards of provision must be carefully tailored to the demands of low-income residents. Poor people can and will pay for services they regard as essential; in practice, today, they often already pay more than the rich.[2] But low-income people will neither pay for nor physically contribute towards the development of infrastructure from which they receive no benefits. This is obvious where there is no infrastructure despite a charge being included for it in plot fees; but it is also true where there is too much infrastructure (such as is evidenced by unused roads, for example) or because of high standards and the resulting unbalanced distribution.

The importance of demand and the communal nature of infrastructure services create a need for institutionalized participation by residents in the planning of investments

- to define appropriate standards;
- to reduce implementation problems, particularly in neighbourhoods where new infrastructure disturbs existing houses;
- to determine realistic levels of charges in relation to costs.

Participation can help not only in improving a neighbourhood's infrastructure; it also helps reduce city management problems that contribute to unbalanced infrastructure provision in the first place. There are many reasons why infrastructure investment tends to be lopsided, inadequate, and involves too high standards. Planning of infrastructure is usually a heavy-handed top-down affair based on inadequate guesses about needs. Vested interests besides those of the users have an especially heavy weight in top-down planning: appropriate infrastructure often does not make for equally lucrative contracts (both officially and unofficially) as high-standard infrastructure does. Officials, too, in the top-down systems are guided largely by their professional training and middle-class values, which make them feel uncomfortable in planning infrastructure at lower than conventional standards and with the people instead of for the people.

5.2.3 HOUSES

If government agencies play the enabling role in developing land and infrastructure, then construction of houses is an activity in which residents, individually, collectively, or through small contractors, are usually much more efficient than any governmental organization. This is so essentially for three reasons:

- families themselves obviously have the best perception of their own shelter needs and their willingness and ability to pay for these;
- very often informal building techniques and practices exist which satisfy effective demand for shelter reasonably well;
- construction by a government organization usually implies additional overhead costs, often in the region of 25 per cent of direct construction costs.

Consequently, the scope for government intervention in this area is limited. Where an enabling strategy has to absorb the bulk of scarce government resources just to develop enough land and infrastructure for low-income housing, intervention in house-building should be directed at further increasing the efficiency of the existing delivery system; government efforts should support the efforts of the urban poor themselves. This is an important point to make, because its acceptance forces governments to study the existing delivery system first before determining areas of intervention. In doing that, one can usually identify some of the following areas for supportive actions:

- introduction of more efficient techniques, very often only a slight modification of techniques traditionally utilized;
- provision of a 'core' house in sites and services schemes or otherwise provision of an appropriate starting point (e.g. only a roof) for families newly on site;
- widening the range of housing designs (and prices) for people to choose from;
- setting minimal functional rules, particularly related to health and fire hazards, governing plot utilization, design and building materials;
- expanding the supply of building materials;
- stimulating the development of adequate financing mechanisms.

5.2.4 FINANCE, ORGANIZATION AND EMPLOYMENT

These aspects have already been touched upon in the earlier paragraphs. Outside support in these areas is crucial to enabling housing strategies. Finance is necessary to acquire land, develop infrastructure and build houses. The poor usually have no access to formal credit mechanisms and often end up paying more for credit than the rich, or being deprived of it altogether. This is where outside organizations, governmental as well as private, have a supporting role to play in more efficiently mobilizing resources for low-income housing.

A variety of schemes is possible depending on the socio-economic context. Long-term financing for the elements discussed in the previous three sections may be provided in one package or separately. The discussion on secure land assumes an added dimension if a clear land title is necessary as collateral for long-term finance. Other ingenious mechanisms may be used to reduce financial problems, such as differential land pricing or stimulating plot owners to sublet or re-sell part of their plots (Thailand 1981: 7; Ward 1981: 39–50). Where direct cost recovery through long-term finance is unfeasible or unreasonable, governments may consider indirect cost recovery, particularly through property taxation.

In sites and services, where it is not always possible to develop new sites close to existing low-income employment centres, there may be a need to bring employment to the new housing areas. This raises issues of industrial incentives, stimuli for cottage industries, services, matching skills of residents with labour and demand, lifting credit bottlenecks for small businesses. If slum upgrading is also perceived as trying to reduce un- and under-employment, then some of these issues must also be addressed in an upgrading context.

This is not very easy as low-income families' employment is usually characterized by a mixture of regular and irregular work, both inside and outside the neighbourhood. The irregular nature of low-income employment makes location all the more important: easy access to the casual job market is vital − if one lives too far away, one hears about such jobs too late to get them. Therefore an unattractive location not only increases transport costs to jobs, but also cuts off access to part of the relevant labour market. The inside-the-neighbourhood nature of low-income employment makes mixed land uses mandatory, at the cost of loss of employment, if this cannot be built into project design.

5.3 Policy formulation problems

A policy expresses a certain preference of ordered events. Such a stated preference provides for checking possibilities on the actions of organizations and individuals. Policy measures designed to facilitate self-help housing often meet with resistance on two counts:

1 They are often a departure from previous practices and as such make the proposer and implementor more vulnerable to possible criticism than a continuation of previous policies. As enabling policies are increasingly carried out in various countries, this resistance will decline, particularly as it becomes possible to see successful examples of implementation in comparable settings.
2 They often reduce the power that certain individuals enjoyed under previous policies. This would hold for any new policy. It will be less serious a barrier to change in a situation of stability and continuity of government, in which the bureaucracy is relatively secure. However, if the governmental situation is unstable, this aspect of policy change is bound to create a lot of resistance in agencies that have focused on house construction.

Such general built-in resistance is compounded by the fact that effective policies in support of self-help housing invariably affect many government departments, often with overlapping areas of jurisdiction and conflicting objectives that become more pronounced when housing agencies start developing land and infrastructure on a large scale. These departments in turn are also subject to pressures of vested interests of outside parties (particularly from the larger firms in the construction and building materials industries).

Moreover, an enabling housing policy inherently banks on the ability of the urban poor to help themselves. This often conflicts with predominant perceptions of policy-makers in a bureaucracy, who, by virtue of their professional background and administrative experience, generally underestimate this capability. At best they feel the poor have to be guided, at worst that the poor have to be prevented from carrying out their innately mischievous acts. Often policy-makers drafting housing policies have never themselves been inside a slum. This lack of actual knowledge of how slum life is organized certainly does not contribute to the formulation of imaginative policies. This is generally aggravated by the fact that professional salaries and fringe benefits in the private sector are substantially more attractive than in government service, which tends to draw the more talented and imaginative professionals away from the housing policy formulation area.

Fortunately training institutions in the housing field, both at the undergraduate levels (particularly in architecture and planning departments) and at post-graduate levels have also devoted increasing emphasis to enabling housing strategies and the role professionals of diverse academic backgrounds may play in these. Moreover, in many Asian countries government leaders, whether civilian politicians or army generals, have come to realize that such strategies, particularly slum upgrading, may be highly popular among the urban poor and could credit the leaders with substantial political dividends. Thus, it is perhaps not so surprising that a large number of governments in Asia with widely diverging political ideologies and different degrees of actively functioning democratic institutions have gradually adopted housing policies supporting self-help during the past decade. Examples range from the military martial law government of General Zia-Ul-Haq in Pakistan and the military-backed government of President Suharto in Indonesia to the Marxist-dominated state government in West Bengal, India.

At this level, however, another problem arises: politicians rarely appreciate the complicated nature of enabling housing strategies, and sometimes, in their drive for quick and popular results, take policy measures which may have harmful side-effects on the implementation of self-help strategies in the long run. Policy pronouncements related to land tenure regularization in slums by Prime Minister Z. A. Bhutto of Pakistan and his successor in power, General Zia-Ul-Haq, have tended

to disregard the complexity of such a policy. Likewise, the Ceiling on
Housing Property Law of Sri Lanka (passed in 1973 to limit the number
of properties an individual could own) was not based on a sufficient
understanding of how this would affect low-income housing supply and
land tenure regularization efforts. (For more about these and other
examples see Angel 1980: 39–50.)

5.4 Planning and implementation

Planning and implementation of any government-sponsored housing project is generally a slow process, because of manpower constraints in the
planning organization and government regulations governing plan
approval, tendering procedures, construction supervision and disbursement of funds. At a time of high interest rates and rising construction
costs, delays in this process tend to be extremely costly. For instance, if
construction costs increase by 20 per cent per annum and the interest rate
is 15 per cent per annum, a delay of one year midway during construction
could easily lead to a 17–18 per cent increase in overall construction costs.
While self-help housing projects avoid at least some of the delays that
characterized conventional projects, the enabling strategy itself is subject to its own species of planning and implementation bottlenecks.
Government bureaucracies are often insufficiently attuned to the different planning and implementation activities and procedures necessary in
such projects. This applies particularly to upgrading, where thorough
physical as well as socio-economic surveys of the project area, including
registration and establishment of conventional property lines, are often
indispensable. In the Karachi Metropolitan Corporation (KMC) for
instance, no surveying capacity for such surveys is available for its large
upgrading schemes, so the work has to be tendered to consultants, which
results in delays due to approval procedures (moreover, the quality of the
work in surveys carried out under contract is difficult for KMC officers
to control, and survey errors subsequently discovered during regularization planning lead to further delays). Attempts to develop a departmental surveying capacity failed due to the rigidity of the KMC
bureaucracy, even though savings in costs and increased accuracy could
be demonstrated by an example of such a departmental survey carried
out in one sizeable slum area (Yap Kioe Sheng 1981). Although smooth
implementation of slum upgrading schemes makes residents' participation in planning mandatory, it is none the less difficult to realize,
because the inherent mistrust between slum dwellers and the implementing agency has to be overcome. This takes time and sensitive
planning officials who are prepared to embark on a protracted dialogue

with the community concerning the upgrading plans. In Karachi, this is particularly difficult: the mistrust has a long history, the planning department has insufficient staff, and motivation of the planning staff suffers because of the insensitivity of senior officials to the problems faced by their subordinates.

A similar problem arises in the field of inter-departmental co-ordination. Depending on the administrative set-up in a particular country, this may be largely a matter of internal co-ordination (such as in the case of KMC in Karachi, where most problems are encountered in co-operation between various KMC departments and in decentralization of KMC activities) or a problem of co-operation between various agencies (as in Bangkok, Colombo and Madras, where the initiating planning agency for upgrading does not have responsibility for substantial elements of the implementation of the projects). Either way, such co-ordination problems give rise to delays and cost escalation. Problems are particularly pronounced in the following areas:

1 *Land matters.* The planning agency rarely controls the project land even if it is in government hands. Provision of land titles to project residents implies that land has to be acquired by the planning agency or that the (private or public) landowner embarks on issuing titles. Negotiations on such issues often take many years. In Karachi leases are issued by KMC, whereas most slum land is owned by other government bodies who are reluctant to lose this potential source of revenue. Disputes on land transfers between the organizations concerned delayed implementation of projects substantially (Wegelin 1981). In Bangkok, increased security of tenure is generally not provided by the main implementing agency, the National Housing Authority (NHA), but this is negotiated with the landowner (in many cases another government agency, such as the Crown Property Bureau or the Treasury Department). This not only leads to delays, but in some cases to the total impossibility of carrying out projects in any meaningful sense (Thai Khadi Research Institute 1981: 9–15). In Colombo, housing units acquired under the Ceiling on Housing Property Law are vested in the Commissioner for National Housing, whereas the planning agency is the Urban Development Authority, and implementation of physical upgrading is the responsibility of the Common Amenities Board. This split of responsibilities has effectively prevented transfer of titles to the residents (DHV 1980: 12ff.). Often, implementing agencies opt for the easy way out by concentrating on lands already under their control. While it makes good sense to initiate new strategies such as slum upgrading and sites and services

schemes on land where clear titles can be issued to the residents immediately, this obviously limits locational choice and, in the longer run, the number of projects that can be implemented.

2 *Implementation of infrastructure upgrading.* Apart from the fact that planning and implementation is often handled by different bodies, it sometimes also happens that different bodies are responsible for different infrastructure elements. This applies most commonly to water supply, sewerage, electricity, health and education facilities. A typical example is provided in the upgrading of Tondo, in Manila, where the water supply and sewerage lines already provided under the National Housing Authority's upgrading programme cannot yet be connected to the greater Metro-Manila water supply and sewerage networks because under the expansion programmes of the Metro-Manila Water and Sewerage System, Tondo is only to be connected in 1982–3. At present, this has resulted in untreated sewage from Tondo being pumped into Manila Bay and 'temporary' water supply at extremely meagre *per capita* provision levels from deep wells dug in the project area. In KMC's upgrading programme in Karachi the problem is different. Minor elements of upgrading projects must be approved by the chief engineer before they can be implemented, and financial procedures are equally centralized under another department, with the result that payments to contractors are generally so much delayed that few contractors are interested in tendering for KMC jobs. Those who do take a job frequently back out after partial completion. In such cases re-tendering is necessary, generally resulting in further delays and cost escalation. Education and health facilities are almost everywhere the responsibility of education and health departments, respectively, whose expansion programmes are rarely in tune with upgrading plans of housing or local authorities, often resulting in delayed provision of such facilities.

3 *Socio-economic programmes,* such as provision of day care centres, training, production centres, small-scale business loan programmes. Here the essence of the co-ordination problem lies in the fact that housing authorities generally have only a faint idea of what could be done in this area, which other organizations could be helpful, or how these organizations could play a role in the overall upgrading programme. This is compounded by the fact that potentially useful organizations in this area are often voluntary, non-governmental organizations with little patience for bureaucratic procedures. As a result, socio-economic components are often weak or, as in Karachi, virtually absent. (Relatively well-co-ordinated examples are available in the slum and shanty improvement programme in Colombo and the slum improvement programme in Madras.)

These problems affect upgrading from the start, and in sites and services, though generally less prevalent or non-existent in the implementation phase, arise once schemes are occupied.

5.5 The post-implementation phase

As noted in the previous section, many co-ordination problems which become clear in the implementation phase of a slum upgrading scheme often only surface in the post-implementation phase in sites and services schemes. Only when residents have been permitted actually to move into such schemes, it becomes evident that co-ordination of housing activities with employment policies is essential. Mismatches in this regard occur regularly even in schemes which are otherwise relatively well-organized (consider, for example, the two-way commuting process between Manila and Dasmarinas New Town Project, skilled labour being in short supply among project residents, many of whom travel daily or weekly back and forth to their unskilled jobs in Manila).

Only when non-occupation was persistent in the Metroville-I sites and services project in Karachi, did it become evident that lack of co-ordination between the Master Plan Department of the Karachi Development Authority (KDA), responsible for planning the scheme, and KDA's implementing departments had resulted in long-term land speculation; bulk water supply would not be provided to the attractively located project area for several years to come, and plots had been allocated largely to home-owning middle-class people instead of to the low-income families for whom they were intended (Khan and Mirza 1981; Siddiqui 1981).

Such co-ordination problems are often important hurdles in the development of successful sites and services projects. The problems are not impossible to overcome, but require a well-co-ordinated planning effort right from the start; the sites and services programme in Madras shows clearly that if there is sufficient goodwill and understanding of each organization's role, effective projects can be developed (India 1981). The interesting feature in planning in Madras is that all concerned agencies are consulted in planning decisions, most notably the Madras Corporation, and the Madras Metropolitan Water Supply and Sewerage Board, which are not involved in implementation, but which are responsible for ultimate maintenance of infrastructure. Planners also brought in at an early stage the Small Industries Development Corporation (SIDCO), nationalized banks, co-operatives and other voluntary community development agencies.

There has been a tendency for governments to be too heavily involved in the technical and physical aspects of building houses and to neglect those areas where outside support is vital, such as the supply of building materials and development of suitable finance mechanisms. The reasons for this are very similar to those leading to inappropriate infrastructure as described earlier. One additional reason applies: government professionals dealing with housing are predominantly architects and engineers with sociologists and economists taking a back seat. This has contributed to an intervention pattern which is not compatible with the efficient implementation of enabling housing strategies.

Many institutional problems surfacing in the post-implementation phase result from insufficient appreciation in the planning phase that the project is not completed after construction of government-provided elements. Future home extension or improvement, maintenance and payment collection are usually taken for granted during planning, resulting in many problems later on. Sensible and sensitive home improvement assistance schemes are needed to enable residents to extend their core houses or build on open plots, and this requires careful planning beforehand, appropriate building extension rules, financial mechanisms and the development of suitable channels of communication between residents and the agency controlling building.

In the area of long-term finance for the residents, there are usually two main issues:

1 The issue of collateral or guarantees (possibilities range from small loans secured on the borrower's character to government-guaranteed mortgage loans with land and structure as collateral).

2 The organizational issue. Loans to residents in a self-help scheme are usually comparatively small, hence the problem of disproportionate overheads arises. This is one of the reasons why commercial banks are rarely interested in financing such projects. Another one is the prospect of large default rates. This means that the brunt of long-term financing is often borne by a government development agency, which is generally ill-equipped to handle such issues. Sometimes a special bank or a community organization such as a savings and loans association or a credit union is set up. Such organizations are potentially useful to mobilize residents' resources precisely because they are close to the residents. Consequently, formal collateral may not be needed and overheads can remain low. However, it takes time and effort for such organizations to mature to a stage at which they can efficiently handle credit for low-income households.

Maintenance is invariably a problem, particularly such routine government responsibilities as collecting garbage, or cleaning drains and sewers. Sometimes the local authority refuses to take over responsibility from the implementing agency, and sometimes all potential for community action in this area is neglected entirely.

Payment collection and coping with arrears and defaults are delicate problems which can only be solved by a client-oriented approach, using rigid enforcement only as a last resort. Because no one anticipates these problems, agencies end up with *ad hoc* solutions, ranging from ignoring difficulties (with severe adverse consequences for project cash flow and replicability) to inconsistent evictions.

Other institutional rigidities are found in rules governing resale, subletting and room renting. This again is generally caused by ignoring such issues in the planning stage and often results in *ad hoc* adoption of regulations which are difficult to enforce.

One may well ask: if most problems result from inadequate planning, why are planning procedures not improved? In some cases they actually are (as in Madras, where building regulations and standards were relaxed and where the maintenance organizations were brought in at the planning stage after an initial project had met with difficulties in handing over maintenance responsibilities). In other situations, lack of understanding or perceived vested interests, or both, prevent the necessary co-operation.

It is clear that a policy shift towards enabling strategies not only requires additional specialized training for employees in implementing agencies, but also changes in employment policies of such agencies. Increased recruitment of social workers in the slum upgrading office of the National Housing Authority of Thailand and the establishment of a Community Development Wing in the Tamil Nadu Housing Board in Madras are steps in the right direction.

5.6 The role of outside donor agencies

The spectrum of outside donor agencies ranges from large multilateral institutions such as the World Bank group, UNICEF and other organizations within the UN system, regional donor institutions such as the Asian Development Bank or the Inter-American Development Bank to bilateral assistance organizations and voluntary agencies. Within this spectrum, the large multilateral institutions, notably the World Bank, have probably been most successful in influencing Third World housing policies and programmes over the past decade. Other institutions generally did not have or did not use as much financial leverage to move governments into the direction of low-cost enabling housing strategies and away from conventional low-cost housing approaches. With the shift in perceptions of the low-income housing problem in the World Bank during the late 1960s and early 1970s and its concomitant lending policies, the World Bank exerted influence in a direction more compatible with supporting activities carried out by smaller donor agencies, most notably voluntary donor agencies supporting voluntary agencies in Third World countries, which generally operate effectively at the project level. The new World Bank approach was also broadly in line with directions advocated by an increasing number of housing professionals, many of whom are engaged in technical assistance projects in Third World countries (Grimes 1976; World Bank 1975). The past decade has witnessed a growing harmony in advocating new directions in housing policies which, overall, made the donor agency system a fairly effective catalyst in increasing acceptance of enabling housing policies and facilitating their implementation. However, this general, positive assessment does not mean that there have not been many pitfalls on the road to effective assistance in self-help housing. Several of these are described below.

Very often existing local agencies (particularly municipalities) which would be logical vehicles in implementing low-income housing policies have been found lacking in implementation capability due to staff shortages, bureaucratic rigidities and a backlog of prior responsibilities. The World Bank's response has often been to support the creation of new development organizations (examples are the Madras Metropolitan Development Authority, the Calcutta Metropolitan Development Authority and the National Housing Authority of the Philippines). While this has sometimes been an effective strategy (such as in Madras), it often added to the plethora of government organizations operating in the low-income housing field, generally with overlapping responsibilities, leading to counter-productive inter-agency rivalries rather than co-operation. It is difficult for a donor agency to exert a positive influence here. One alternative could be to try to work out organizational responsibilities between agencies, staffing levels and procedural arrangements in substantial detail during project assistance negotiations, to be supplemented by monitoring and evaluation consultants during the implementation and disbursement schedule of the scheme. Client organizations, however, do not generally like such paternalistic arrangements. Because donor agencies value a good working relationship with their clients (with more possibilities of persuasion) and because of the 'spending pressure' discussed below, there are clear limitations to the hard-nosed negotiation approach.

Donor agencies generally are under pressure to spend funds. In the competition for funds between agencies and, within an agency, between departments, a shortage of 'bankable' projects to utilize the available allocation would reflect badly on the agency's staff, and it might lead to reduced allocation in subsequent years. Donor agencies are susceptible to such pressures to different degrees. It is encountered most strongly in the official bilateral programmes, where 'showing the flag' in a completed project, combined with direct interests of donors' national consultancy and supplier firms, reinforce these pressures. Multilateral lending agencies have more countervailing controls in their international management structure. That their funds originate to a large extent from the international capital market further modifies the interests they represent. The client organizations in Third World countries are often quite aware of this spending pressure and make use of it, sometimes by playing off one donor agency against another.

Thus competition tends to undercut donor agencies' effective ability to insist on institutional reform or otherwise unpopular conditions such as granting solid land titles to residents in slum areas or raising property tax rates to ensure cost recovery. Admittedly, there are instances where lending agencies prefer non-funding to funding of projects if they believe institutional conditions for success are insufficiently secured. The decision of the World Bank in 1977 not to go ahead in funding the Lyari slum improvement project in Karachi was certainly sensible from that point of view, although it was a painful decision in view of the substantial amount of preparatory work carried out by both World Bank and local staff. The increasing tendency to establish aid consortia for individual countries may lead to a more objective assessment of programmes and projects, limiting the potentially harmful impact of donor competition on the implementation of effective housing strategies.

Often an entirely different pattern is encountered, however. A group of committed individuals in government institutions can sometimes use the leverage of potential foreign assistance to realize policy changes or organizational reforms necessary for the successful implementation of enabling housing strategies. The establishment and expansion of the National Housing Authority of Thailand's slum upgrading programme have come about through application of such leverage, and similar tactics have been successfully applied in relation to the housing programme in Sri Lanka.

Many early problems in funding slum upgrading and sites and services schemes originated in insufficient appreciation on the part of donor organizations of the specific environment a project or programme has to function in. As donor agencies increase their experience with such projects, their sensitivity also improves. It is now realized how much effort must be spent on sector reconnaissance, project preparation and technical assistance during implementation to ensure programme continuity.

This applies particularly to large multilateral donors, which can afford to retain adequate staff to handle such specialized issues. For bilateral and voluntary agencies this is more difficult.

Voluntary funding agencies generally function best in their role to fund activities of an experimental or innovative nature carried out by non-government organization (NGO) in the country concerned. Innovation is generally not the hallmark of housing bureaucracies in Third World countries, but there is often sufficient flexibility to follow successful implementation of pilot projects by NGOs or to integrate their activities within the framework of government projects or programmes.

5.7 Summary and perspective. Will enabling housing strategies survive in the face of institutional problems?

The common strands identified in the previous sections as causing institutional problems in implementing enabling housing strategies consist of attitudinal problems, vested interests (including corruption), inadequate organizational ability generally rooted in typical poverty problems such as abysmally low staff salaries, and inadequate funds for simple support activities.

Foreign donor agencies have generally been a positive force in the change of housing policies and implementation of effective enabling strategies. The question that remains is: can conservative attitudes, vested interests and organizational deficiencies be overcome in the long run? If the experience in the past decade is any guide, the answer to this question should be a cautious 'yes'. Enabling housing strategies, after all, are increasingly being implemented despite such bottlenecks. The donor agencies have been pushing with the tide, because there really is no realistic financial alternative to benefit substantial numbers of an ever-growing poor urban populace and the growing awareness of this among bureaucrats, professionals and politicians alike. Nor has the popularity of upgrading and, to a lesser extent, sites and services been lost on politicians.

These factors in turn will also help to change organizational structures where these are counter-productive, but the power of vested interests will exercise substantial resistance to such changes. Against such resistance, many governments and implementing agencies have already changed directions in their housing policies in a remarkably short time period and are slowly but continuously improving on their performance in supporting initial self-help projects. Specialized training programmes, as well as information exchange and dissemination projects are important supporting elements in this process of change. This gradual transition in most urban housing programmes in Asia, particularly in cities such as Manila, Madras, Calcutta, Colombo and Bangkok, means that guarded optimism may be the concluding note of this chapter.

Notes

1 The term 'slums' does not denote a single type of neighbourhood. In the Asian context, slums in Bangkok tends to refer to areas where people have rented land on informal contracts of less than two years' duration. Most houses in slums are owner-occupied. Slums in Sri Lanka are one- and two-room publicly owned tenements, while 'shanties' refers to self-help houses on squatted or rented lands. In Bangkok, some slums do not have houses of poor standards; in Pakistan, slums generally means high-density neighbourhoods with predominantly poor-quality houses, either owned or rented by their residents, and either built by self-help or conventional structures converted to 'slum use'.
2 For example, water vendors are very much in evidence in Karachi's slum areas, but virtually absent in higher and middle-income areas, which are served by the municipal water supply system. Municipal water charges are computed as a percentage of assessed (1968–9) property value. On a per gallon consumption basis municipal water charges are insignificant compared to the prices charged by the vendors.

References

Angel, S. (1980) 'Land tenure for the urban poor', paper presented to the World Congress on Land Policy held at the Lincoln Institute, Cambridge, Massachusetts, 23–27 June.
Churchill, A. *et al.* (1980) *Shelter*, Washington DC, World Bank Basic Needs Series.
DHV Consulting Engineers (1980) *Second Progress Report, Colombo Slum Upgrading and Shanty Improvement*, Colombo, Urban Development Authority.
Grimes, O. F. (1976) *Housing for Low-Income Urban Families: Economics and Policy in the Developing World*, London, Johns Hopkins University Press.
India (1981) *Case Study of Construction Management in Villivakkam Scheme and Estate Management in Arumbakkam Scheme*, Madras, Madras Metropolitan Development Authority and Tamil Nadu Housing Board.
Khan, A. R. and Mirza, M. I. (1981) 'Metroville I', paper presented to the Seminar on Sites and Services in Asia, National Housing Authority of Thailand, Bangkok, 5–16 January 1981.
Siddiqui, Islamuddin (1981) 'The implementation of the Metroville-I project in Karachi', in J. J. van der Linden *et al.* (eds) *Between Basti Dwellers and Bureaucrats: Lessons in Squatter Settlement Upgrading in Karachi*, Amsterdam, Vrije Universiteit.
Thai Khadi Research Institute (1981) *Summary of Preliminary Report of the Evaluation of Slum Upgrading Activities of the National Housing Authority, Phase I*, Bangkok.

Thailand (1981) *Seminar on Sites and Services Schemes: Exploring the Asian Experience. Seminar Conclusions and Recommendations*, Bangkok, National Housing Authority of Thailand.

Ward, P. M. (1981) 'Financing land acquisition for self-built housing schemes in developing countries', *Third World Planning Review*, 3 (1), February.

Wegelin, E. A. (1981) 'The economics of land tenure regularization in Katchi Abadi Improvement', in J. J. van der Linden *et al.* (eds) *Between Basti and Bureaucrats: Lessons in Squatter Settlement Upgrading in Karachi*, Amsterdam, Vrije Universiteit.

World Bank (1975) *Housing Sector Policy Paper*, Washington DC.

Yap Kioe Sheng (1981) 'Problems in implementation', in J. J. van der Linden *et al.* (eds) *Between Basti Dwellers and Bureaucrats: Lessons in Squatter Settlement Upgrading in Karachi*, Amsterdam, Vrije Universiteit.

6
Community participation: its scope and organization

R. J. SKINNER

6.1 Introduction

This chapter is an attempt to identify the major difficulties arising in the incorporation of community-level participation in upgrading and sites and services projects. This is considered important because, while problems clearly appear in most such projects, there has been no comprehensive attempt to ascertain why. Many studies have been undertaken on rural community development problems (see, for example, Holmberg 1952; Huizer 1963, 1971; Lewin 1972; Nimpuno 1975; Van Velzen 1972) and these can provide valuable insights into the urban process. But, to date, urban problem analysis often comes down to clichés and rationalizations of failures (for example, residents are apathetic or lazy, do not know what is 'best' for them, or do not have the time to participate). While there is some truth to be gleaned from some of these views, they do not really provide a basis upon which to make participation effective. A clear understanding of the origins of the problems is, therefore, essential. This chapter will seek to provide this by investigating not only specific project difficulties, but relating these to the policy and planning processes behind them, the way in which projects are implemented, and the reaction of the target populations. A range of country examples will be given, many of which are referred to in the notes to be found at the end of the text.

To be of value in improving the degree of participation in future projects, the chapter cannot stop at the stage of problem identification, but will provide some recommendations as to methods by which the difficulties identified can be overcome.

6.2 The policy context of participation

There are a host of reasons why community participation can be deemed desirable in self-help projects. From the point of view of the project agency or ministry these may include:

1 the saving of the agency's scarce manpower resources and thus expenses by having a community organization to undertake tasks it would otherwise have to do itself (especially in labour and maintenance);
2 promoting social development by increasing local self-reliance;
3 making political capital by demonstrating the people and the government are working hand-in-hand;
4 increasing political or social control by co-opting a strong but manipulable community leadership;
5 maximizing the efficiency of project implementation by giving the community organization those functions which it can often fulfil better than the project agency (e.g. determining what local improvement priorities are, persuading residents to participate and policing collective activities);
6 ensuring that by establishing a strong community organization, the project area continues to develop even after the withdrawal of the agency staff; the organization will determine and undertake new projects which it will be able to implement and manage largely on its own.

Such reasoning can sometimes disguise paternalism on the part of the agency. Where it is seen that the agency needs to reduce its expenses and that the provision of affordable housing for the poor is dependent upon this, the emphasis of the argument will be to convince residents that their co-operation and giving of ideas will enable planners to produce plans which are for the community's benefit. Participation is then a moral obligation for residents to assist the 'experts'. It might also be argued that participation will eradicate the marginal character of a settlement's residents by transforming them into 'solid citizens' working for planners who have the welfare of the poor at heart. The advantages of participation seen in this way are to perpetuate an unequal relationship between the agency and residents with participation facilitating the implementation of projects rather than genuinely seeking to increase the decision-making power of the poor.

As for residents, some of the main benefits they may perceive in participation can be listed as:

1 cheapening of project costs and, therefore, repayments they have to make;

2 ensuring that the improvements which are made correspond to their priorities (if participation includes the planning stage);
3 with an organization which persists after the withdrawal of the official agency, the chance of establishing some local autonomy in development with reduced dependence on outside agencies;
4 for community politicians, participation may provide the basis for local power in the community organization and the fostering of patronage relationships with city politicians.

Of course, not all the apparent advantages described above will be felt equally by all governments, planning agencies and residents, but there do seem to be sufficient reasons to make participation an attractive *prima facie* proposition. So, to what extent has it been incorporated in self-help projects to date? In later pages I intend to illustrate the wide potential scope for community involvement as demonstrated in certain projects which have been implemented. At this point, however, I prefer to indicate the policy and planning constraints which largely determine the extent to which projects in a particular country will include participation.

First, while participation may appear desirable, it is an area in which many countries have little experience. This is reflected in the lack of suitable personnel (e.g. social workers and community organizers), and the working approaches of professional staff who have been trained in conventional housing techniques which involve little, if any, popular participation, and have little idea how to incorporate it in their planning. Specific difficulties here might include the resistance of contractors in working with self-help labour, the uncertainty of completing projects 'on time', and the reliability which can be placed upon residents undertaking their tasks fully or with sufficient competence. As I argue later, this need not prevent participation being sought, but it can make planners hesitant about entering what is a new and risky field.

Secondly, the nature of the government concerned is of crucial importance. It may consider popular organization as dangerous to its political control and, therefore, either eliminate participation completely or restrict it to very small project elements which produces participation in construction but leaves aside the social and economic spheres; participants are mere 'contractors'.[1] Furthermore, a government closely tied to construction and building materials manufacturing interests will subordinate participation to those interests. So, for example, where materials standards are set so high that they can only be met by formal sector producers: there is no scope for the participation of the informal sector or groups of residents producing their own materials.[2]

I have considered the advantages of community participation and the major general policy and planning constraints upon incorporating participation into projects. I shall turn now from the policy to the project level, showing the potential scope of participation and problems in obtaining community involvement. In both of these areas some of the policy-oriented questions mentioned above will reappear, but in more detail.

6.3 The potential scope of community participation

Sites and services and upgrading projects to date have seen community-level participation in such diverse spheres as financing and payments collection, materials production and distribution, maintenance, planning, employment generation, estate management and health care, apart from the perhaps more obvious sphere of collective labour. Some of these I shall return to later. The point at this stage is that participation appears potentially feasible in just about every activity in a self-help project. That this is not usually the case in practice in most projects raises the question of what defines the real boundaries of participation in a specific scheme. I shall consider this question in two parts; the determination of boundaries by relatively 'objective' factors such as the project type and its components and, secondly, subjective factors which emanate from the project agency or government and the target population. This distinction is purely heuristic and it will be seen that the objective and subjective always interact or overlap.

The type of project dealt with is important in determining the potential scope of participation. It is a truism that upgrading areas are more conducive to collective action than sites and services areas. But this crude division masks important differences within these categories, notably that of sites and services. The advantages of upgrading areas for participatory practices can be broadly stated as follows. They involve already established populations who will often have developed their own systems of internal interaction and organization over a long period; these 'social networks' can be seen not only as support mechanisms, but as contributing to the creation of social cohesion based on trust, knowledge of one's neighbours and experience of co-operation.[3] With these sub-systems of co-operation already in existence, and especially if they have developed into a community level organization which has experience of collective action, it is often possible to envisage incorporating residents' participation into the upgrading programme at an early stage (such as the initial planning of the project).[4] It may also be that houses, though of poor quality, may be considered by residents as temporarily adequate and therefore relatively higher priority is given to social facilities like clinics or schools; in these fields participation, if there is to be any, must be collective (unlike house-building, which is essentially individual). The existing organization in the settlement can, therefore, be involved in a broad range of activities, apart from house construction, from a relatively early stage.

On the other hand, it is usually assumed, sites and services areas are particularly resistant to collective participation because they lack the above characteristics. Residents are new to each other, they have no experience of co-operation with one another, and their initial concern will be to construct a satisfactory house. While accepting these points in general, I reject their universal applicability. Precisely why becomes clear if one considers the different types of sites and services project which can exist. I shall classify them as follows:

– open application schemes (new sites with plot application open to all);
– overspill sites for upgraded settlements;
– relocation sites for eradicated central slums or squatter settlements;
– group application schemes.

Open application projects mix families with no previous contact or organization. Here indeed one will find a population who are strangers to one another. If collective activity is successful, it is likely to take a long time and thus exclude large parts of the initial planning and implementation phases. As I shall argue later, this will reduce the chances of securing participation in the maintenance phase also.

In overspill projects, families will have been members of the same community and could, therefore, be expected to translate their old ties and relationships to the new site. This is particularly so if residents displaced from the upgrading area are regrouped geographically on the new site in a similar distribution to that which they occupied in the old area. One might therefore expect that co-operative action, other things being equal, would be more feasible in such a case and at an earlier stage.

Relocation projects could have characteristics similar to overspill projects, but relocation itself hampers participation. Although families would carry their previous collective experiences with them to the new site, they may well also harbour a hostility to the project agency since their former homes will normally have been demolished against their wishes. This would leave them unlikely to agree to co-operate with the agency in the project's development. Moreover, since sites and services plots are invariably more expensive than the previously occupied houses, and are often located further from employment sources, many of those moved will prefer not to take up the offer of a serviced plot. Thus, the original population will have been depleted, and social cohesion reduced as surplus plots are occupied by outsiders.

The fourth category, group application schemes, refers to such projects as co-operatives acting to secure plots collectively for their members (for Tanzania see Guhr, chapter 4). When the group is itself composed of 'strangers', such as certain types of co-operative are, the result is likely to be similar to that described for open application schemes. But if it is, say, an employment-based co-operative where members have worked together and decided upon the collective approach themselves, one can expect this to be more likely to produce communal activities.

If this brief comparison of project types does not convince the reader that some sites and services schemes are more conducive to participation than often believed, one example may serve to change his mind. In Lima in May 1971 some 9000 families who had recently squatted on public and private land were relocated on the outskirts of the city.[5] The new area, named Villa El Salvador, was laid out in plots and only minimal services were provided (unsurfaced roads, and street lighting at the entrance to the settlement). By April 1976 the population had soared to over 130,000. It is clear that no previous co-operative experiences could be carried over into the new area, residents were strangers to each other, they had been evicted (after violent clashes with the police) from the area in which they were squatting, and since not even a wet cell was provided in the new site there was a need to concentrate initial efforts on individual house construction. Although these factors would all suggest the impossibility of obtaining communal participation in the project, precisely the reverse was observed. After five years of existence, a community organization elected by residents was involved in the following range of activities, amongst others: the identification of land speculation by plot occupants; securing internal financing for collective projects through a self-managed community bank (plate 6.1); disseminating information in improved hygiene and nutrition practices through a community health centre; running a small bus service; selling key building materials at controlled prices; funding a construction company which served as a contractor for groups of residents building meeting halls or other community level structures; creating employment by establishing a clothing workshop.

If such an array of participatory practices was so rapidly evident in a settlement which was apparently conceived in such a way as to preclude even the most elementary forms of participation, one clearly has to look beyond the variable of project type to understand the sources of

Plate 6.1 Community bank in Villa El Salvador, Lima, April 1976. Built and operated by residents, this gave loans for collective projects, such as a medical centre, bus purchase and meeting halls.

Plate 6.2 Trawk Ton Mamuang, Bangkok, June 1981. Normal slum upgrading practice of limiting participation to minor spheres such as fire control. Fire extinguisher case used as notice-board to list community association's self-determined activities and expenditures thereon.

Plate 6.3 Trawk Ton Mamuang, Bangkok, June 1981. Playground built by residents with state-provided materials.

participation. A starting point would be the Lima project mentioned above. The most salient explanatory factors in this case are:

1 The project agency (and the ministries with which it co-ordinated) gave popular participation a great deal of prominence and generated expectations from the population of its effectiveness (for example, the official agencies were believed to be sincerely concerned that settlement development be determined by residents themselves).

2 From the outset it was clearly stated that there would be no 'gifts' from the state. Development was dependent on local efforts, and the state would support these efforts.

3 The participation sought from residents was comprehensive: it was to include physical improvement, employment generation, and would thus provide channels for social mobility, and the organization which residents ran would contribute not only to local but national development (see also point 8 below). In other words, the population was given a 'carte blanche' to do whatever and however much it considered necessary.

4 Initial successes of the collective experience increased community self-confidence and laid the ground for further ideas and efforts.

5 Although the project agency and associated official bodies had promised a great deal of co-operation at the start, they later defaulted on

these (e.g. refuse disposal trucks, loans for school-building, delayed individual water connections) so that residents were forced to provide as much as they could for themselves. Their earlier successes gave them confidence to take up this challenge.

6 Certain of the residents' leaders had previously had experience of organizing the poor (through political activities).

7 From the outset the project agency set about establishing a structure of residents' representation.

8 In 1971 Peru as a whole was passing through a period of social and political change under a government which propounded an ideology of participation and mobilization in all popular sectors (industry, agriculture, etc.) This later developed into a popular movement in which labour and peasant unions became important political actors and with which low-income residents' organizations were able to ally and receive support.

Of course, the above all points to a case peculiar to this one country at that particular time. But it is still possible to deduce certain generalizations from the experience which can be applied elsewhere. I see these generalizations as divisible into two categories, that of the approach used by, and constraints imposed upon, project agencies and, secondly, the interdependency of project components which can determine the likelihood of collective participation. These categories require some explanation.

Certain details of project agency approach will be dealt with in the next section; here I am concerned with overall strategy. The first and most obvious point is that the agency immediately set about organizing the population, making it clear that participation was a pre-requisite of development and even official assistance. This compulsion to organize, and agency commitment to stimulating organization, is usually lacking in sites and services schemes and often in upgrading projects; partly this reflects the agency's inexperience in the sphere, but probably stems more from a lack of confidence in the people's own abilities or an unwillingness to share control, both locally and nationally.[6] In such cases 'participation' may be declared as an objective but in practice amounts to organizing residents under a leadership which is in the pay of the state and serves to control its constituents (Eckstein 1977: 78ff.; Michl 1973: 170–3). But even in countries committed to popular participation at the national level little, if any, provision is actually made to stimulate grass roots involvement.[7]

Next, the project agency needs to avoid arousing residents' fears that they are simply being exploited as cheap labour. Where residents are brought into decision-making as well as implementation, this is more likely. Moreover, it reduces the chances that the people will feel that all implementation aspects are 'the agency's responsibility'. This attitude, one of dependency on the state, is fostered by agencies who take all decisions and direct residents to follow them; the same agency may then complain that residents are not willing to participate, thus creating a self-fulfilling prophecy.[8]

A major constraint on agencies wishing to follow the approaches proposed above is clearly political. Where participation and local control are feared by national governments, agencies themselves are trapped. But my point is that even regimes advocating participation do not provide the political or financial support to make it practicable at the project level.[9]

Turning now to the point of interdependency of project components, I shall refer to relationships between project components themselves and the connection between these and the wider political system. In the Villa El Salvador case residents were involved from the planning stage. But when decisions are made from outside and residents' views not respected (perhaps the decisions actually conflict with local preferences) then it becomes less likely that participation in the implementation and maintenance stages can be obtained.[10] To this extent participation in one stage of a project can be said to depend on participation in another.

Interdependency has other facets. If the population is made to feel its views are genuinely influential then there can be beneficial 'spin-off' effects. For example, if it is clear that development is dependent upon local initiative and action, the residents themselves are charged with the project's success and will have an incentive to make it successful – they cannot simply blame the project agency. Similarly, if an initial participatory venture is successful, it can lead to more commitment, enthusiasm and self-confidence for further activities to be carried out.[11]

The Villa El Salvador case demonstrated two additional forms of interdependency, one locally based and the other national. The first derived from the comprehensive nature of the project, which included employment generation, social facilities, physical improvements and local political power (popular organization and decision-making). Certain projects demanded that residents had some control over all these spheres. So, for example, the desire to start community-owned firms to provide employment was put into practice through the ability of the organization to obtain funds from its own bank. Some projects eventually failed precisely because the state later limited the extent to which local decisions could be taken and success in one area depended on success and participation in another. For example, the community built a central clinic and paid for it with its own bank loans. But authorization to sell medicines was not given by the Ministry of Health; this cut income for the clinic, which was forced to default on its loan repayment, causing liquidity difficulties for the bank. The project agency and co-ordinating ministries need to be aware that successful participation often depends on linkages of this kind which are broken when there is no possibility of communal decision-making in this sphere, or there is an obstruction introduced by an official actor.

The other type of interdependency is national in character. The Peruvian case in which the government propounded an ideology of social change through popular mobilization legitimized and stimulated settlement organization and produced organizations in other spheres which added to the effectiveness of settlement activities.[12] Most countries are not going through a similar process but one can still make the point that much local participation will depend on national government provision of a suitable framework which permits it to operate. The clearest needs in this respect are laws which give rights to community organizations to effect their decisions and give them legal backing (e.g. the existence of criteria to approve residents' organizational structures and give them legal recognition which permits them to sign binding collective contracts with state and other bodies for communal improvements, and loans, etc.)

In this section I have attempted to show that the sphere of potential participation by residents is almost unlimited. What defines the practicable degree of participation in any given case in any particular country will be the type of project concerned, the official conception and commitment to participation, and approaches used by project agencies, including the identification of necessary interdependencies of spheres of participation, and the support received from national governments in giving a legal and political framework conducive to the growth of residents' participation. I now wish to move from a consideration of the parameters of participation to problems which often emerge at the project level, and to suggest explanations for these.

6.4 Participation at the project level: problems of implementation

In this section I shall make use of evidence from urban sites and services and upgrading projects, and supplement these in the text and notes with data gathered from rural areas which reveal features of relevance in assessing urban problems of participation.

A common complaint of project officials is that residents are apathetic or lazy. This is more likely in upgrading projects than sites and services because in the former some degree of collective participation will often have been built into project plans so that if it fails to materialize such an accusation can readily be made. In sites and services, however, plans are usually comprehensively designed for all stages of the project by the planners and therefore little participation is expected. My view is that the urban poor care very much about their living conditions and anyone who accuses them of laziness ignores the long hours of labour they put into often poorly paid employment, looking for jobs, or steadily building up their temporary shacks into liveable accommodation. If this view is correct, the question is why, if they are not apathetic or lazy, they often refuse to co-operate with project officials by giving part of their own labour, funds or organizational skills.

One reason may be that they do not want the project in the first place or, at least, not on the terms presented by the agency. This can be explained in a variety of ways. If, as often happens, the plans for the improvement of an irregular settlement are drawn up by planners without consultation with the intended beneficiaries, there is a strong chance that the plans do not correspond with residents' wishes. They may well want an improvement in their settlement but have different priorities to those held by planners. Officials, brought up and educated in a middle-class value system, are unlikely to share the same view as those facing problems of poor housing every day. Indeed, it is the latter who know what the problems really are. Thus, a project which aims to provide a good road system, a modern market and new secondary schools will meet with little satisfaction from dwellers who are mainly concerned to gain access to cheap permanent materials for house-building, clean water and health facilities for their children. In the meantime, roads are a luxury, existing market stalls are acceptable, and secondary schools are less important than primary education or training for employment. It would, therefore, be irrational for residents to co-operate in such a project; at best, they can be expected to accept it as inevitable.[13]

Another rational reason for rejecting plans is the cost involved. Most planners today are aware of cost implications of improvement projects and attempt to assess the payment capacity of the population. But residents are not likely to feel obliged to pay, even if they can, for improvements they do not regard as priorities. The result may be low rates of cost recovery and another reason for the agency to believe that the poor are not worth trying to improve. But, again, it is vital that some attempt is made to ascertain 'felt needs' if repayment ('participation in financing') is sought.

The above is related to another problem in obtaining participation – that of residents rejecting new, cheaper materials (e.g. self-made, soil-cement blocks) or the forms of organization demanded of them in the envisaged participatory programme. Again, rejection can be seen as perfectly rational. In situations where cement blocks or bricks are well-known for their durability, it would take an irresponsible person to accept an outsider's suggestion that he uses a new, unknown material. He would, I feel, be best advised to wait longer to buy the more expensive material which he is sure will conserve his limited savings in the largest investment he will make in his life. Similarly, he may know that hiring a mason to build for him is costly, but experience tells him that the house will not collapse. To tell him he must join with neighbours to make their own blocks and then build their houses together can only be received as an invitation to folly by a reasonable man. What is needed in both cases (that of new materials and innovative construction organization) is a major effort of demonstration that the planners' proposals can work. Laboratory testing and evidence that in other countries these practices have proved successful mean a lot to the technician, but nothing at all to the resident. Demonstration houses (preferably occupied), on-site tests of new materials and tours by residents' leaders or respected individuals to other areas which have successfully used the new technique are a few of the methods by which the community may be convinced to take part in the project.

In some cases, however, the agency will simply have to accept that residents do not want to employ the new material and are unconvinced of the value of mutual efforts. The only wise course is then to abandon these proposals and seek to modify plans on the basis of what residents do want.[14]

It is worth briefly discussing another often-held view that the urban poor are too 'ignorant' to understand the complexities of a housing development project. As with many middle-class perceptions of the poor, this view demonstrates professional ignorance of the clients who are supposed to be served. The Villa El Salvador case shows that a formally 'uneducated' population can establish and manage such complex institutions as a bank, a materials store and a cultural centre using audio-visual equipment. The Lusaka upgrading experience has shown that residents can guide planners (not vice versa) in such apparently 'technical' operations as road routing (Martin, chapter 3). Ignorance, therefore, seems to be far from endemic. What is indisputable, however, is that the poor are often unfamiliar with, and lack sufficient understanding of, the proposals which are brought to them by project officials. The partly employed construction worker cannot be expected to be 'au fait' with loan conditions, the calculation of interest rates and the meaning of grace periods; the office cleaner is unlikely to be able to interpret house plans. But planners who are sufficiently interested to attempt to explain these have found that residents have a remarkable learning capacity.[15] If treated as intelligent individuals, they are more likely to participate in the project than if dealt with as inferior beings (Huizer 1971: 390). It is my suspicion that the labelling of the urban poor as ignorant, apathetic or lazy is used by many project agencies as a reason for 'bulldozing' a project through, half-heartedly perhaps inviting participation, and treating the resultant hostility encountered as justification and verification of their initial assumptions. While these almost slanderous opinions may often be genuinely held, they no doubt also often reflect the agency's inability to conceive of planning and implementation approaches which they cannot find written in the standard planning texts. Moreover, a 'top-down', bulldozer approach gets the project completed quickly; it is then for the residents and estate managers (not the implementation agency) to pick up the pieces in terms of high repayment costs for unwanted facilities, high default rates on repayments, poor local maintenance, increased hostility to the housing authorities and even perhaps vandalization or non-utilization of facilities provided.

It is precisely this approach of implementation without consultation that produces a form of dependency amongst squatters or sites and services plot holders. Where everything has been decided and often largely implemented by the agency, it is understandable that residents consider all improvement and maintenance tasks as the responsibility of the authorities. Moreover, not only may they refuse to participate in terms of labour but also in terms of payment, expecting costs to be borne by the state – 'the state wanted the project so should pay for the privilege'. The more schemes are implemented in this way, the more they will serve as examples in later project areas for residents to refuse to participate in what increasingly becomes defined as a state responsibility.

The above pages may have given the impression that planners are to blame for all failures in participatory projects. In fact there are a few more criticisms I shall make later of approaches which diminish the likelihood of popular co-operation, but first I prefer to consider some constraints on participation which really do appear to emanate from the target population itself.

One of these is that the low-income groups of whom we are talking are far from homogeneous. Any one settlement may contain not only a wide range of income groups but differences in tribe, religion or ethnic group, any of which can mitigate against attempts at collective participation. Tribal groups may not be willing to work with neighbours from other tribes, for example. In the Asawasi housing estate in Kumasi, Ghana, residents who had migrated from the same part of the country congregated together and had little contact with other ethnic groups. It did, however, seem that a basis for collective action existed since each group had its own leaders and, therefore, an inbuilt organizational structure with which project officials could have made contact. This is particularly likely since chiefs, as in this case, are respected individuals with the authority to mobilize their tribal members. Where they are convinced that a particular project will benefit their members, they may be a powerful mobilizing force. Moreover, in urban areas the power of chiefs is often tending to decline and an improvement project may offer them the opportunity to shore up their legitimacy.

Of course, this implies that contact will have to be made separately with each tribal group, avoiding the problem of genuine community-wide co-operation. This presents a dilemma: should one attempt integration of groups which have traditionally chosen to remain separate, or should one capitalize on the internal cohesion of each group separately? This is equally true of differences based on religion, and there is no simple answer which applies to all cases. In some instances of community development internal divisions of this kind have even been used to the advantage of all by presenting the improvement project as a competition between the different groups, thus giving a stimulus to each group to perform better than the other.[16] And where divisions are non-conflictive, there may be no reason to interfere with existing social patterns. But when integration is a goal, the kinds of projects upon which this could be based are those which are strongly wanted by all groups and which the project agency clearly states can only be provided by collective efforts (e.g. a school or clinic specializing in child care).

Another form of internal differentiation is that of income. This is a potential problem of community participation because there will sometimes be differences of interest and scaling of priorities between the groups concerned. For example, the poorer groups may prefer a local meeting and recreation hall or improved health facilities, while the richer (being able to spend their leisure time and obtain medical care outside the settlement) may place more emphasis on improved roads − if some have cars − or playgrounds for their children. To me this implies the following. For upgrading areas, the priorities which are followed should be those of the majority, which will not include the relatively well-off. This is for two reasons: if collective action is sought, it is essential to obtain the support of the majority, and secondly, the relatively rich are not as much in need of additional facilities as the poor and may well have more alternatives to satisfy their requirements (such as the outside medical care already mentioned). For sites and services areas I would argue against the mixing of income groups and for establishing settlements with different standards corresponding to the paying capacity of their own income groups, and allowing the priorities of these groups to be expressed free from the intervention of the conflicting interests of different income groups.[17]

Another internal constraint upon community participation derives from residents' suspicions and distrust of the project agency. It may be suspected that the call for participation is just a disguise for exploitation of residents in producing more cheaply what otherwise the state would have been obliged to provide. This point has already been mentioned in an earlier section, but here I would reiterate that this becomes less likely when residents are made to feel that their actions in the sphere of decision-making are as important as that of implementation – and are therefore largely determinants of the activities required in implementation – and I would add that the extent to which such suspicion is felt will often depend on previous experiences they have had of the activities of official agencies.[18] The second point underscores my earlier claim that low-income residents are very rational actors. In such an instance much of the time of the agency must be spent in showing that it has no relationship with its predecessor (assuming this is so) and in convincing residents of the value of the new proposal. Nevertheless, it may ultimately be necessary to withdraw from the settlement and move to another, in the hope that successes in neighbouring areas will have a demonstration effect on the first.

Suspicion, however, may be based on other grounds. Huizer (1963), for example, described how Central American villagers refused to participate in an irrigation project because they feared their work would eventually only produce improved irrigation for their hated landlord. In urban areas the landlord can also often be the beneficiary of upgrading projects. Improvement efforts can leave tenants, who have been required to contribute their labour and savings to the project, facing increased rents calculated on the basis of the improved properties. Resistance to participation in such cases can only reasonably be expected to be overcome if the state demonstrates its commitment to residents, rather than landlords, by compulsorily transferring ownership rights to occupants.

Another source of opposition to participation can be found in residents' fears that the project agency or state is seeking to take over existing organizational arrangements. In Latin America this is often interpreted in political terms: agencies, who are ultimately servants of the state, impose conditions for their support which undercut extant power relationships, or seek to co-opt local leaders in an attempt to mobilize the population as a whole behind the project, which has political purposes as much as physical improvement goals. In Africa and Asia, on the other hand, this is often a matter of threatening the position of established and locally accepted traditional leaders.

Where the project deliberately sets out to replace these arrangements there is little useful to say here. Where this is not the manifest intention, a few comments can be made. The first is that an attempt should be made to determine the hierarchy of authority which exists and make initial contacts through those at the top of the pyramid. Although this does not guarantee that leaders will be willing to co-operate, it does offer the possible economy of only having to persuade a relatively few residents of project benefits which, if successful, will be operationalized through the existing system of authority and mobilization without having to employ mass communications techniques. For cases in which local suspicion is that of political control, there are two possible approaches which can be adopted. The first is similar to that already proposed – to channel project ideas through settlement leaders. The second applies when residents suspect project benefits will include a 'rake-off' to a corrupt leader who is being bought off by the state in order to get the project implemented. Here the agency has the opportunity to give itself legitimacy in the eyes of residents, by showing that it is attempting to respond to popular wishes rather than collaborating with unwanted leaders. This is a somewhat complicated matter but boils down to holding meetings with residents as a whole, supplemented by house-to-house visits in which project aims are explained. Of utmost importance is the rapid establishment of a formal elected organizational structure for decision-making and implementation (which may be of a very simple form to begin with) in which existing leaders will have to compete with any other candidates. The more residents want the improvements offered by the project, the more likely they are to respond to such a challenge to unwanted domination. Making the improvement project dependent upon a formal, elected organization (supervised, perhaps, by the agency in such cases) is a further stimulus to the population and a tool which they are able to use to displace local despots.[19]

A problem which appears to be related is that which Roberts (1973: 256) has called delegation of authority by 'public symbol'. This means that in populations where the members do not have sufficient knowledge of each other to be able to evaluate leadership qualities, members tend to elect those who display characteristics which would seem to make them suitable leaders for such reasons as their contact with official institutions. Thus, social workers or teachers, for example, living in the settlement, although not typical of the population as a whole, are projected into leadership positions. The newer and larger the settlement the more likely this phenomenon is, and the more likely to persist (e.g. in sites and services schemes). While this may present no difficulties in terms of getting the project run and the community organization under way, there are certain disadvantages. The first is that this does not really represent popular participation in decision-making and reflects a general lack of confidence in being able to make decisions. This not only falls short of self-determination, which may be a goal, but also hints at a wider lack of confidence which may later manifest itself in an unwillingness to participate in collective activities which residents feel they do not have the ability to undertake. Secondly, there is an inbuilt tendency to overload those elected by public symbol, not only in decision-making but also in practical tasks like fund management or labour organization, so that collective works are not effectively implemented. Such a situation should not be regarded too pessimistically at the start of a project – at least agreement has been reached on collective participation and respected leaders elected. But for the reasons given above, efforts should be made to instil confidence in the 'ordinary' resident that he or she can take over these functions. This implies training programmes in whatever spheres are relevant for the project (e.g. building group supervision, stores management, elementary hygiene education, and so on). In this the project agency may well be able to count on the leaders elected by public symbol who want to divest themselves of some of their burdensome responsibilities. Roberts, at least, who coined the term 'public symbol' after investigation in Guatemala City, found that it could be combated effectively by such action (1973: 256–60).

This section does not claim to be exhaustive in its treatment of project-level problems of securing community participation; it does however, I believe, deal with many of the major difficulties likely to be encountered. If the approaches advocated above are accepted they provide a framework of thinking which can be usefully applied to other specific day-to-day problems which may be faced in a particular scheme. I wish now to turn to a consideration of the implications of the previous three sections for general project orientation, which will also suggest problem-solving approaches.

6.5 Implications for project agency approach and organization

Anyone who has read to this point of this chapter probably assumes that community participation is a desirable feature of upgrading and sites and services projects. Equally probably the main concern of the reader is to determine why it is often so difficult to obtain effective participation in such projects. If the arguments and examples I have put forward are convincing it should be possible to accept the general proposition that participation in most cases is viable and is potentially limitless in its scope. The problem is how to make it work in practice. In this section I shall suggest how modifications in the approaches and organization of project agencies can contribute to making it work.

For, there is a tendency to create an artificial division between sites and services and upgrading projects in terms of their potential for residents' involvement. But the distinction is really one of degree rather than inherent and immutable differences. I have shown that participation can be extremely successfully employed in a sites and services scheme. Undoubtedly there are more difficulties in sites and services areas, but this means that, if we remember the benefits of participation, more effort should be made to generate it rather than abandoning the attempt from the outset. My view is that many project officials steer away from the problem of participation whenever possible; they feel more at ease with schemes over which they have full control. Sites and services give them the excuse they seek: since they are new settlements, they can be easily treated like conventional low-cost housing estates and the problem of participation can be side-stepped ('whoever heard of participation in a housing estate?').

If participation is to be generated, however, other prejudices need also to be overcome. One is that planners are the only people who can, or have the right to, plan. As I have argued, not only can low-income residents plan (which in the Lusaka case cited required no training and in the Villa El Salvador case only basic education in book-keeping for the bank), but they need to be involved in planning if they are seriously to be considered as participants in implementation and, even more so, in maintenance. This is what I referred to earlier as the 'interdependence' factor.

This itself implies another change of attitude − that of seeing residents as capable of involvement in many more aspects of project development than providing labour (which often boils down to using them as cheap subcontractors). This attitude even exists in agencies which espouse 'community development' as an integral part of their projects.[20] This restricted approach is quite logical if settlements are conceived of as purely physical entities (in which people happen to live). In this case, the project is 'technical' and has no social character. There are certain ways in which a project can be designed and constructed, and people 'participate' by following these predetermined plans.

But, as I have tried to show in section 6.4 settlements are complex social organisms and to ignore this makes it impossible to understand why people do or do not participate in any given project, or why projects are sometimes rejected by their supposed beneficiaries. An understanding of this, moreover, can only come when the project agency starts from the assumption that resistance to participation is *rational* from the point of view of the residents. Only if this is accepted – and indeed it is reasonable to assume that people act in ways they see as in their best interests – can an enquiry into the reasons for resistance be made, and steps be taken to combat these.

Planners, architects and engineers are not usually trained to be able to make such enquiries or undertake the social actions required to convince residents that they would benefit from participation in a project. Problem identification and attempts at their solution, therefore, require skills often absent from project agencies. These are the skills of the sociologist, the social worker, or the community development officer. Probably one of the biggest mistakes made in self-help programmes has been the attempt to undertake them with essentially the same type of staff as would deal with conventional housing projects. Self-help programmes, however, are different and require additional manpower to confront the different problems involved.

The introduction of new manpower and the attempt to understand local social organization and cope with residents' problems and objections throughout the life of the project implies spending considerable time on interviews, meetings, demonstrations, and so on. Obtaining people's views, determining their priorities, explaining the project to them, training them in certain project tasks, and dealing with problems which arise in the participatory exercise are only some of the time-consuming elements which a self-help project will impose on the agency. It must, therefore, be accepted that participation demands time and patience. This will be frustrating for the official who evaluates project efficiency in terms of speed of execution of pre-defined implementation stages. But this can be myopic. Although much time will be spent in the early parts of the project, in generating participation, this can pay dividends later when the agency is able to reduce its manpower commitments and thereby reduce costs by handing over to the community organization tasks which otherwise it would itself have been obliged to take on – maintenance, loan repayment collection and the construction and management of community facilities are only a few of the spheres which have been communally taken over in upgrading, sites and services and village improvement schemes in various countries.[21]

None of the above implies that planning loses its importance in self-help programmes; quite the contrary – it assumes more importance, although the form it takes will of necessity be different. First, it will have to be flexible; an agency may have plans which it presents to residents but, if participation and co-operation is sought, it must be willing to adapt these plans to coincide with community preferences. This in itself presents a challenge to planners who will need to revise their initial designs, not once but, perhaps, many times. The most difficult planning task, however, lies in the dynamic nature of participation itself. Participation can never be precisely planned. Hoped-for participation may not be forthcoming; in other cases new opportunities for participation may unexpectedly arise. The planner, however, is not redundant. Certain expectations (perhaps only hopes) can be used as initial indicators of project elements which could form the basis of participation. As already mentioned, this might be the involvement of an elected group of residents in deciding where roads should be routed in an upgrading area, as in Lusaka. In a sites and services project the first collective action might be the building of a school, as in the Villa El Salvador case in Lima where schools were identified as a major priority by residents. Whatever the project, a certain degree of 'planning for participation' is necessary, although this will invariably need to be revised in the light of experiences gained in the particular project area. A guiding principle, however, is that initial expectations should be low, the agency advocating (and only advocating) collective projects which are relatively simple (and therefore more likely to succeed) with a view to these early successes laying the foundations for more adventurous collective activity later.[22] What this means is the adoption of the principle of 'phased participatory planning' – a new concept which revives the role of the planner in self-help projects.

Finally, it must be envisaged that the time may come when many of the project agency's functions can be taken over by organized residents themselves. New developments for the area will be decided upon, and implemented and maintained, by the community. This will certainly not always be achieved (though the Villa El Salvador case is one in which it was) but where it is, adequate provision must be made to allow it to continue effectively. This means the establishment of a legal or contractual framework which enables the community to act as a legal entity. Without this there can be no collective contracts and no negotiations which carry any authority with the concerned public or private agencies. The community will, therefore, remain dependent on state agencies to contract and negotiate on its behalf. This is ultimately a political decision which is outside the direct control of the project agency. The agency, however, can be an advocate of such a policy and this, perhaps, is the real test of its commitment to participation: is it prepared to place itself in the position of arguing that a participatory project's success is proven only when a community is locally self-governing and not a mere appendage to the 'real' authorities promoting the scheme?

146 PEOPLE, POVERTY AND SHELTER

Notes

1 An example of the narrow scope participation can have is the Tondo Fore-shore Upgrading Project in the Philippines. When started residents were invited to select one of three prepared plans for remodelling (or 'reblocking') in each designated block, help each other with the removal of houses subject to relocation under the reblocking process, improve their own houses and maintain them, and to keep streets clean. Project and reblocking plan design, infrastructure installation, the determination of the level and type of services, and most maintenance functions are the preserve of the National Housing Authority, together with the World Bank, private contractors and public servicing agencies. It is relevant here to note that Tondo's upgrading resulted from strong resistance by various community groups to a 1974 government plan to eradicate some 70 per cent of residents' dwellings.

2 For further discussion of the state serving business interests in low-income housing projects see Pradilla (1977: 44–8) and Burgess (1982: 71–85). In projects in Indonesia the state housing corporation, Perumnas, designed low-income projects with a core house to be extended with particle board which can only be supplied by a large factory and which supposed beneficiaries neither liked nor could afford. This material was in fact no superior to traditional bamboo; allowing the use of wood would also have allowed local, small-scale production (personal communication).

3 Studies of such social networks and local relationships of co-operation include Gutkind (1965; 1967), Perlman (1976: 196–7) and Wee (1972).

4 A clear example of this is the Road Planning Groups of Lusaka's upgrading areas as described in chapter 3 by Martin.

5 For a fuller analysis and description of this settlement see Skinner (1982).

6 In Nairobi, for example, one planner privately admitted that his team had never tried to incorporate participation while their public reasons were that people were 'not interested' in participation. Here, and in the case of the Malawi sites and services programme, participation was no doubt also feared for the wider political repercussions which might emerge when people felt they could exercise authority (personal communications).

7 Tanzania is a case in point. Although the single party system provides for cells of ten houses, headed by a local party leader, in all urban settlements, and these are supposed to be the centres of residents' collective action, minimal training of leaders results in negligible community involvement in either sites and services or upgrading areas. This problem is compounded by the fact that the Ministry of Lands, Housing and Urban Development, co-ordinating the programme, has only one community development worker on its staff – and his post is named 'technical assistance officer'; it seems almost ashamed of appointing such a professional (personal observation).

8 It might be objected that sites and services areas need to be planned before occupation and that, therefore, consultation is impossible. At best such a view demonstrates lack of imagination. Projects can be planned which leave room for later developments on the basis of the population's own expressed preferences (e.g. is an additional school needed before domestic water connections, or playgrounds before surfaced roads?). This was the approach used in the Lima case cited above.

9 It could be argued, not unreasonably, that some countries in this category simply do not have finances to train local leaders or community development staff for this purpose (e.g. Tanzania). But others, like relatively rich Tunisia, which in its own terms is 'socialist' have no such excuse. In Tunis, the Djebel Lahmar upgrading project excludes all local participation in decision-making. The reason given is that residents are adequately represented by party leaders and elected municipal officials. In practice, however, the district planning office makes the decisions and the other 'representative' bodies merely acquiesce (personal observation).

10 On a visit to the Manzese upgrading area of Dar Es Salaam in 1978 an engineer explained to me how all planning and implementation decisions had been made without local consultation. He then expressed dismay that residents failed to repair broken facilities such as standpipes.

11 This implies that the project agency seeking to create such self-confidence should consult with residents to advise on initial ventures, with a view to identifying those which are relatively simple, and giving as much support to it as possible without appearing to be the dominant partner. Thus, a relatively high initial investment in technical assistance may be required, but will be repaid through good co-operative relations with the agency in a successful venture, and self-reliance by the community later. The degree of assistance can probably then be phased out (see Skinner 1980).

12 An example in the Lima case was being able to link with peasants to set up a direct food supply system, cutting out intermediaries with economic advantages to peasants and residents.

13 Even if planners are convinced that the main need of an area is, say, a good sewerage system to prevent the spread of diseases, while residents claim they want domestic electricity, the decision cannot be forced upon the community if participation is sought. A classic community development technique in such a situation would be to accept the residents' goals, help them achieve them, and by doing so create a relationship of trust ('the agency cares about what we want'), which can then be used to convince residents that the sewerage system is in their own interest. For a successful example of this approach in Egypt see Ross and Lappin (1967: 15–17).

14 Rejection here may also be due to status considerations. In the Asawasi housing estate in Kumasi, Ghana, dwellings were extremely cramped and a local research institute advocated extensions by means of stabilized laterite soil blocks. Although there was no real effort to demonstrate their viability to the population, it was clear in a series of interviews I undertook in 1977 that residents preferred to wait and save longer to buy scarce and expensive cement blocks. This was largely because they were seen as representing a 'real' house in status terms. One Ghanaian colleague suggested to me that the only way laterite would be accepted was if the government used the material in its future housing estates – which was highly unlikely since it shared the same status perception.

15 Examples can be found in Nimpuno (1975) for Dodoma Region, Tanzania, American Friends Service Committee (1975) for Kafue, Zambia, and Angel and Phoativongsacharn (1981) for Bangkok, Thailand.

16 There is debate amongst community development workers, however, on

whether this is desirable, since divisions may be deepened. Furthermore, when dealing with diverse groups like this, much care and diplomacy has to be exercised to avoid accusations of favouring one tribal or religious group over another (Arensberg and Niehoff 1971: 127–8).

17 I am aware of arguments against this proposition. First, it could be claimed that, by mixing income groups, the better-off can be made to cross-subsidize the project costs of poorer residents, as is currently practised in Malawi, for example. But it takes little imagination to see that, if there are distinct income-based sites, the richer group sites can be made to cross-subsidize those of the poorer. Secondly, conventional social housing planners argue that socio-economic mixing has the advantage that the poor try to emulate their richer neighbours and thereby produce better quality housing. Here I would make only three criticisms of this (although there are many more): first, this assumes the poor do not know what they want and the rich know what is 'best' for the poor; second, it is debatable whether the poor should be encouraged to invest their meagre incomes in emulating those who can afford relatively luxurious housing; third, the real reason why mixing is advocated (to be generous) is that where the richer live, more facilities will be provided. But this can be a burden on the poor, who cannot afford these and, in any case, is more of an indictment of the system which provides to those who already have than a genuinely socially conscious argument.

18 An Indian engineer told me of a proposal he had to introduce a new, cheap roofing system to a slum neighbourhood in Madras. He felt two major obstacles confronted his scheme: first, the idea was new and would have to be proved before residents could be expected to adopt it; second, and more importantly, there had been a previous attempt to build improved housing which, designed by an expatriate 'expert' completely unfamiliar with the local climate, proved uninhabitable because inadequate attention had been paid to cross-ventilation. Previous negative experiences of this sort are generally accepted as perhaps the major hindrance to an agency gaining credibility with the populace (Hyman et al. c. 1966: 96–8).

19 Two Indian architects with whom I spoke about a proposed improvement in which they were involved felt this was likely to be the most successful strategy. Existing leaders had been accepted because they provided marginal benefits, but their decisions on behalf of the community were often determined more by self-interest (e.g. bribes) than any concept of a 'common good'. Nevertheless no alternative programme of substantial benefits existed which gave an incentive for residents to organize against their entrenched leaders. With the improvement project the control of investment, savings and the course of development were expected to be large enough to prompt residents to ensure they were self-controlled, rather than resting in the hands of an untrusted leadership.

20 One Tanzanian official, for example, responsible for 'community development' in the national upgrading and sites and services programme defined the concept as state planning and provision of infrastructure and community facilities with residents' participation limited to house construction. Here 'community development' was simply conventional project construction which, it was assumed, meant the 'community' (seen in purely physical terms) was being 'developed'.

21 Abrams (1966: 187–8) describes how rural communities in Ghana were successfully given collective responsibility for recovering official roof loans from their members. Construction, management and maintenance of community facilities by residents are described in American Friends Service Committee (1975) and Nimpuno (1975).

22 The reader is again referred to the Kafue settlement in Zambia, where such a process developed: initially limited house-building participation grew into the collective production of communal facilities like schools (American Friends Service Committee 1975). Similarly, in the Villa El Salvador case, participation started with assisting the army in levelling roads and developed into school-building, clinic construction and management of a community bank.

References

Abrams, C. (1966) *Housing in the Modern World*, London, Faber & Faber.

American Friends Service Committee (1975) *Chawama Self-Help Housing Project, Kafue, Zambia*, Philadelphia, American Friends Service Committee.

Angel, S. and Phoativongsacharn, Z. (1981) *Building Together: Issues in Mutual-Aid Housing*, Bangkok, Asian Institute of Technology, Human Settlements Division.

Arensberg, C. and Niehoff, A. (1971) *Introducing Social Change. A Manual for Community Development*, Chicago and New York, Aldine-Atherton.

Burgess, R. (1982) 'Self-help housing advocacy: a curious form of radicalism. A critique of the work of John F. C. Turner', in P. Ward (ed.) *Self-Help Housing. A Critique*, London, Mansell, pp. 55–97.

Eckstein, S. (1977) *The Poverty of Revolution. The State and the Urban Poor in Mexico*, Princeton, Princeton University Press.

Gutkind, P. (1965) 'African urbanism, mobility and the social network', *International Journal of Comparative Sociology*, 6 (1), 48–60.

Gutkind, P. (1967) 'The energy of despair. Social organisation of the unemployed in two African cities: Lagos and Nairobi', *Civilisations*, 17, 380–405.

Holmberg, A. (1952) 'The wells that failed: an attempt to establish a stable water supply in the Viru Valley, Peru', in E. H. Spicer (ed.) *Human Problems in Technological Change. A Casebook*, New York, Russell Sage Foundation, pp. 113–23.

Huizer, G. (1963) 'A community development experience in a Central American village', *International Review of Community Development*, no. 12, 161–78.

Huizer, G. (1971) 'Community development, land reform and political participation', in T. Shanin (ed.) *Peasants and Peasant Societies*, Harmondsworth, Penguin, pp. 389–411.

Hyman, H., Levine, G. and Wright, C. (*c.* 1966) *Inducing Social Change in Developing Communities*, New York, United Nations, Research Institute for Social Development.

Lewin, R. (1972) 'Matetereka', in L. Cliffe and J. Saul (eds) *Socialism in Tanzania. An Interdisciplinary Reader*, vol. 2: *Policies*, Nairobi, East African Publishing House, pp. 189–94.

Michl, S. (1973) 'Urban squatter organization as a national government tool: the case of Lima, Peru', in F. Rabinovitz and F. Trueblood (eds) *Latin America Urban Research*, vol. 3, London, Sage, pp. 155–78.

Nimpuno, K. (1975) 'Community development and popular participation in Tanzania', Gothenburg, mimeo. Preliminary draft of paper prepared for Regional Habitat Conference in Dar es Salaam, June 1975.

Perlman, J. (1976) *The Myth of Marginality. Urban Poverty and Politics in Rio de Janeiro*, London and Berkely, University of California Press.

Pradilla, E. (1977) 'Notas acerca de las politicas de vivienda de los Estados Latinoamericanos', *Arquitectura Autogobierno*, 7, July–August, 37–48.

Roberts, B. (1973) *Organizing Strangers. Poor Families in Guatemala City*, Austin and London, University of Texas Press.

Ross, M. and Lappin, B. (1967) *Community Organization*, 2nd edn, London, Harper Row.

Skinner, R. (1980) 'Technical assistance in sites and services projects and its relationship to overall project development', mimeo, Rotterdam, Institute for Housing Studies.

Skinner, R. (1982) 'Self-help, community organization and politics: Villa El Salvador, Lima', in P. Ward (ed.), *Self-Help Housing. A Critique*, London, Mansell, pp. 209–29.

Velzen, H. van (1972) 'Staff, kulaks and peasants: a study of a political field', in L. Cliffe and J. Saul (eds), *Socialism in Tanzania. An Interdisciplinary Reader*, vol. 2: *Policies*, Nairobi, East African Publishing House, pp. 153–79.

Wee, A. (1972) 'Some social implications of rehousing programmes in Singapore', in D. Dwyer (ed.) *The City as a Centre of Change in Asia*, Hong Kong, Hong Kong University Press, pp. 216–29.

7
Four experiences with settlement improvement policies in Asia

P. BAROSS

7.1 Introduction

By the early 1970s, orthodox housing policies emphasizing public sector-sponsored construction programmes of finished dwelling units for poor urban families came under increasing stress in many developing countries. The collapse of confidence in the ability of government agencies to solve the 'housing problem' through the rapid development of 'low-cost' housing estates was largely due to their actual performance. While official housing statistics documented mounting shelter deficits, housing agencies were delivering too few units too expensively, and often failing to reach or retain their user target groups.[1] Professor Koenigsberger (1974), a long-time advocate of public assistance to alleviate the housing problem of poor families in developing countries has aptly summed up the lessons of the last twenty years: 'The government should not be in the business of building houses.'

In contrast with the poor performance of the state sector, numerous empirical studies documented the vitality of the owner-managed, popular housing sector which actually houses a large proportion of low- and middle-income families. Often operating under adverse economic, legal and institutional conditions, poor urban families, artisans and small contractors were responsible for the development and gradual improvement of some 30–80 per cent of new additions to the housing stock in the growing cities of developing countries over the last twenty years.[2] This housing activity not only 'solved' the existential shelter need of a sizeable segment of low- and lower-middle-income groups, but had a substantial macroeconomic impact on the various informal sector activities associated with housing. 'Resourcefulness' became the most commonly used adjective to describe the popular or informal housing sector, and the case for absorbing popular efforts into, rather than exclude them from, overall housing strategy was forcefully argued by Turner (1976: 157): 'In an economy of scarcity the mass of common people, though poor, possess the bulk of the nation's human and material resources for housing.'

The convergence of these two, almost universally observed experiences, the evident failures of public housing agencies to respond to the low-income housing need via conventional housing development and the recognition of the positive contribution that low-income families can make in developing their own housing solutions, led to the formulation of a new housing policy paradigm – evolutionary housing strategies. This approach attempts to strike a balance between public resource allocation in the housing sector and the mobilization of family and community resources. Typically, governments' contribution will be a building site (or the granting of title or lease on already occupied areas), infrastructure, credit, and perhaps technical assistance for house improvement, while the responsibility for shelter construction is shifted to the domain of the individual family. The purpose of the evolutionary housing strategy is to support housing development, that is a continuous improvement of the housing stock starting from very low levels of material quality, instead of promoting the construction of finished dwellings in a single construction period.[3]

In general, there are two types of projects implemented within the framework of the evolutionary housing policy: serviced plots and settlement upgrading. In the first type, vacant land on the fringe of the city is acquired by public authorities and developed with basic residential services. Individual plots are then allocated to low-income families who are responsible for developing their own housing. These projects also occasionally provide some initial core structures ('utility wall' in Pakistan's Metroville projects, minimum and sub-minimum houses in Indonesia's PERUMNAS projects, 'shelter shell' in the Philippines, etc.) and finance, technical assistance, or building materials for house construction. More recent generations of sites and services projects attempt to provide a greater variety of plot, services, and shelter options to attract a mixture of income groups and often incorporate sites for industrial and commercial uses to create job opportunities.

The second type of evolutionary housing strategy is implemented in the already built-up areas of a city (centre and transitional zones) with the aim of integrating those popular settlements which in the past have developed outside the legal housing market. These settlement improvement or upgrading programmes typically entail the extension of public infrastructure and social services, some rearrangement of the settlement layout, a degree of tenure legalization and, occasionally, financial assistance for house improvements or small business ventures.

Today, many countries in Asia adopt settlement improvement programmes as part of their housing policy. They are most vigorously pursued in Indonesia, Papua New Guinea, Thailand and the Philippines, where the projects are co-ordinated and implemented by central government housing or urban development institutions. In India there are many varieties of bustee improvement in a number of states and large cities, and the first experiences with shanty improvement are also under way in Sri Lanka (Rodell 1980b). Slum improvement, rather than clearance, has also been accepted in Pakistan, Burma and Nepal although it is carried out on an *ad hoc* basis rather than as a matter of long-term policy. As more policy-makers are prepared to view the upgrading of existing low-income settlements as a rapid and significant contribution to improving the level of housing services to the urban poor, it is important to review the experiences gained from completed or operational projects.

This paper reports on the implementation of low-income settlement policies in the capital cities of four countries in South East Asia – Indonesia, the Philippines, Thailand and Papua New Guinea. The focus is on three project components generally advocated to be the core elements of upgrading programmes, namely the improvement of tenure security, residential service provision and cost recovery. Placing these experiences in the local urban context, the paper starts with a brief description of the historical articulation of low-income settlement formation in each city, and in the concluding part will speculate whether the current policy represents a long-term commitment of public assistance to the prevailing social practices of low-income settlement formation or, on the contrary, is merely one aspect of the overall policy which in fact arises to repress their present developmental form in the future.

7.2 Urban context

Jakarta, Manila and Bangkok typify the pattern of urban growth experienced by many developing countries; they are large, fast-growing, underserviced, and the majority of urban citizens have low-paid, often insecure, jobs. In each city, the officially estimated housing deficits are hopelessly large, and if poor families had not built for themselves, there would certainly be many shelterless rather than merely badly housed people. In contrast, Port Moresby, in Papua New Guinea, is a small city (120,000), but with problems of jobs and housing very similar to those of metropolises forty to fifty times its size. In all four cities neither the formal real estate market nor public housing agencies have developed housing options which are affordable for families with incomes below the 50–60th percentile. The fact that there is no direct correspondence between the demographic size of cities and the size of bad housing areas should be considered by those simplistic-minded planners and policy-makers who believe that controlling urban growth or decentralizing large cities will automatically ease the pressure on the housing market. Rather, the causal variables explaining the size and severity of the housing problem in any city appear to be the rate of urban growth (need), employment and wages (demand), cost and access to housing resources (supply of land, finance, materials and labour) and the discriminating practices of urban governments in providing public services to already-settled locations (urban management).[4]

While the physical appearance of most low-income settlements in the four cities could be described in fairly similar terms (medium to high densities, temporary or semi-permanent materials, inadequate or non-existent public infrastructure and services) they are in fact the product of very different histories. Two aspects of this historical process may be the most decisive – the urban land market and the dominant ideology underlying the promoted forms of residential development. How much land is available for low-income families to start the shelter development process will simultaneously define the locational spread of settlements in the urban fabric, the dominant range of settlement sizes and average densities and crowding. The institutional practice of settlement development promotion influences both the perceived security of investment in shelter construction by the urban poor and the obstacles to providing public services in these areas as a routine municipal responsibility.

The development of low-income urban settlements (kampongs) in Indonesia is closely related to the traditional concepts of land transactions and the historical segregation of Western and native urban development, which was inherited from the Dutch colonial period. After independence, official acceptance of this dualistic urban development principle led to the continuous growth of kampongs which now house some 60 per cent of the population in the large Indonesian cities. The complex set of traditional arrangements which guide the transactions between buyers and sellers, lessor and lessees of land and houses in the kampongs might be confusing to a Western observer, but it is perfectly clear to the people who actually engage in these transactions. The flexibility of the system allows an almost infinite way of scheduling housing investment, from renting room and bed spaces in informal hotels to renting or leasing mini-plots of 10–30 m² and building temporary shelters on them, to buying land and constructing a house which can be enlarged or improved over time. The lack of organized 'formal' subdivisions, at least until the early 1970s, forced practically all income groups to participate in the kampong housing process, enhancing both the social mixture in these residential areas and their legitimacy (Baross 1980).

Similar arrangements are also one of the dominant transactional forms of granting development rights to new migrants to the city in Papua New Guinea (Norwood 1979: 73–85). Customary land holdings which make up much of the land resources of Port Moresby offer members of the local community the possibility of perpetuating traditional housing practices, and also accommodate new migrants who seek land for housing. As the ethnic composition of each 'urban village' is different, so is their linkage with various regions of the country from where the migrants originate. The transactions underpinning village expansion on customary land appear to be simple, cheap and straightforward for those involved. When a member of the local community needs a new plot, the village council will tell him where to build, and he can develop the land without any payment. For a newcomer to the community, the procedure is much the same: he will introduce himself to the village council through the recommendation of some relatives or friends already living in the area, and will then be given a plot to build on, in exchange for nominal yearly payments.

The other emerging low-income settlement formation process in Port Moresby is squatting on unused government land. These settlements are developed by migrants who have no historically established ties with existing local communities, and who, in the absence of other alternatives, build their houses on government-owned land which would be difficult to use for high-standard commercial or residential development. The migrant settlements enjoy a tolerated co-existence with the expatriate-dominated official city, and in the past have received some water supply from the city council.

The various types of low-income settlements in Bangkok represent stages of transformation from traditional to modern (market) land transactions. While the majority of older settlements emerged as people were given permission to build on land owned or controlled by religious and royal institutions, from the 1960s onwards a new type of arrangement has emerged in the form of temporary land rent. Many small landowners in and around Bangkok have converted their land (which was vacant or in agricultural use) to offer small plots to prospective low-income housebuilders on a temporary rental basis. The difficult nature of soil drainage conditions in the city, the abundance of land supply and the low immediate commercial expectations of landowners all contributed to a low-income settlement development process which was both vigorous and semi-legal. The low rental fees and unregulated building possibilities enabled poor families to achieve housing with relatively cheap recurrent charges. While this type of land development is illegal, the fact that people can register their houses with the metropolitan administration and thus obtain identity cards, school places for their children, and so on, lends a degree of legitimacy to these settlements.

While access to land and, to some extent, urban services for low-income house-builders is facilitated by transactions which are dominated by traditional concepts of exchange in Indonesia, Papua New Guinea and Thailand, the transformation of urban land to the market domain has practically been completed in the Philippines. Both the Spanish and American colonial administrations pursued land policies which were aimed at destroying traditional practices, such as land under communal control, and transferring land and development rights exclusively to the private, public or institutional domain. A strong individualistic attachment to private property (and a keen recognition of its commercial value) was entrenched in the major urban centres by the time that massive rural displacement during the Second World War, and city-bound migration due to the neglect of rural development, placed increasing pressures on the capital city's land resources. Land had already been locked into a clearly defined private and public ownership pattern, and was not available for low-income house-builders who were forced to resort to the only other development alternative, squatting. The low-income housing stock in Manila thus evolved partly on marginal land (river banks or estuaries, railway lines, etc.) unsuitable for residential development or on unprotected parcels of private and public land. The latter, in general, are suitable for low-income residential use, although they are designated for other uses by master plans and the prevailing commercial pressure of the land market. Compared with the situation in the other cities, Manila's poor families have the least security over the permanency of their current housing arrangements, a point which was driven home forcefully in the period 1968–75 when some 95,000 families were evicted and resettled on distant sites (Philippines 1975: 17).

7.3 Settlement improvement policies

Governmental programmes to upgrade popular settlements in all four cities exhibit a remarkable similarity in terms of their objectives and programme components. This policy package, in turn, is clearly a derivative of the global technocratic paradigm of recommended action for settlement improvement – municipal service extension, tenure security, capital recovery, socio-economic stimulation and local participation. However, a closer examination of the implementation of the policy reveals differences in scale, emphasis and orientation in each country, which reflects the practical constraints imposed by the varied types of low-income settlement development processes that these policies are supposed to assist, or, alternatively, to discriminate against.

Jakarta's Kampong Improvement Programme (KIP) is chronologically the earliest and in scale the largest settlement improvement effort in Asia. It now extends to some 200 cities in the country. Because kampongs are legitimate, if not necessarily desirable, residential areas, there were no inherent political or legal difficulties involved in initiating the policy. The problems that the designers of the policy were faced with were primarily financial and administrative, that is, where to get the money to provide infrastructure in previously unserviced areas and the technical manpower to co-ordinate and implement the work. After the first five years, the financial problem was eased by an IBRD loan to support the programme, and the shortage of technical and administrative staff was resolved by designing a relatively simple improvement programme with a decentralized implementation structure. KIP thus evolved as a low-standard public works programme of road and walkway construction, some drainage improvement, provision of water through privately controlled public taps and, where land was available, school and health centre construction. In the beginning an elaborate scoring system was devised to identify priority areas for improvement, but political considerations to spread the programme uniformly among the major administrative divisions of the city and the rapid speed with which construction proceeded soon made selection criteria irrelevant. By 1980, an area of some 7380 hectares in Jakarta were involved in the KIP, benefiting an estimated 3.5 million people. The policy emphasizes speed and equality of treatment for all low-income settlements at the expense of depth (inclusion of socio-economic components and tenure regulation) and sensitive adjustment to local conditions. There are, however, two discriminating elements in the policy which exclude certain types of kampongs from receiving improvements. First are those settlements which encroached upon public or institutional property and are thought not to be suitable for residential use (railway rights of way, river banks, etc.). While one can argue with the often unrealistic margins that planners in Jakarta established as unsuitable zones, the zones in most cases are places where it would be difficult to justify the implementation of the standard kampong improvement package. Yet, it is in these areas that the poorest of the city, the newly arrived or temporary migrants, live and that the environmental conditions are the most squalid. So long as these settlements are allowed to remain, their inclusion in some degree of municipal service extension would be desirable. The second type of never-to-be-improved kampongs are those areas which have been designated by the city's master plan for airport extension, infrastructure construction, industrial zones, open spaces, and similar uses. Current estimates place 5–10 per cent of all the kampong areas in the above two categories (Devas 1980: 39).

The evolution of settlement improvement policy in Papua New Guinea corresponded with the overall revision of the general housing policy of the country in 1973, and thus reflects a strong preoccupation with improved shelter production rather than merely infrastructure extension to squatter areas (Papua New Guinea 1975). Incorporating the ideological context of self-assertion of a newly independent country the official policy took a considerably more sympathetic view of the difficulties new migrants face during their economic integration into the city and their corresponding problems with housing than do many other countries in the region. The customary references to squatters and squatter areas are missing in policy documents, and have been replaced by use of the terms 'settlers' and 'migrant settlements'.

The settlement improvement policy stresses three conditions which are seen as necessary to stimulate housing improvement: collective involvement of the residents in deciding the future layout of the community, provision of secure tenure on individual plots, and financial and technical assistance for house construction. A partial financial recovery is planned through the repayment of building material loans and municipal taxation of the developed plots. The policy includes all spontaneously developed migrant settlements on government land, both in Port Moresby and in the other major towns of the country. However, settlements which were developed on customary land are excluded from the current programme because of the complicated land ownership issues involved.

The slum upgrading programme in Bangkok is of more recent origin, representing a shift from the previous policy of rehousing slum residents in government flats to a new policy of upgrading. Again, the announced policy takes a comprehensive view of the needed programme components, stressing tenure security and the inclusion of socio-economic development as the important basic conditions for the programme's success. Yet, it is the land tenure issue which appears to be the most difficult problem to solve in the manner envisaged by the policy (Sidhijai 1980). Neither private, public, nor institutional landowners are willing to make a long-term commitment to the permanency of low-income settlements on their property, nor are private owners willing to foreclose rent increase options once the settlement is improved. In the absence of effective legal instruments, the National Housing Authority (NHA) has to negotiate with each landowner in order to obtain permission to enter the property and undertake physical improvement. Pressed by its own production targets, the NHA was forced to adopt a *modus operandi* which dropped the tenure condition from the slum improvement policy and merely asked for a non-binding agreement from the landowners not to evict the residents in the next five years in exchange for public expenditure on physical improvement. Of the 217 slum areas identified by the NHA only about 97 slums will be upgraded in the next five years, due to difficulties with land tenure agreements. This limited commitment will enable the NHA to give more attention within the implementation process to individual communities than does the KIP in Indonesia, but it will also reduce the effectiveness of the programme in dealing with the overall size of the population currently living in existing and potential low-income settlements.

In the Philippines, the Zonal Improvement Programme (ZIP) has emerged after a difficult process of adjustment between politically organized community demands and official insistence on the viability of prevailing government resettlement policies. The lengthy confrontation over the redevelopment of Tondo, the largest squatter community in Manila, was finally resolved by an upgrading proposal (with limited resettlement on a nearby site) which included all the four elements of the generally advocated settlement improvement policy: secure tenure, municipal infrastructure, socio-economic components and capital recovery. This model, in turn, created the precedent for other squatter communities to demand similar treatment and the policy was extended to cover all of Manila as well as some other regional cities. In 1979, 212 slum areas were identified for upgrading in metropolitan Manila, and an additional 203 'slum pockets', housing some 30,000 families, were recommended for removal. Thus the initial economic and institutional conditions which influenced the location of low-income settlements in the city imposed a serious limitation on the development of an upgrading policy which could redress the tenure and environmental conditions of the spectrum of different types of low-income settlements. The strong orientation towards the incorporation of spontaneous settlements designated for upgrading into the urban land market mechanism is another (less explicitly) stated objective of the policy. This is achieved by the following procedure:

- re-subdivision of the area into individual plots (re-blocking);
- transfer of tenure as an urban asset at prevailing market prices;
- the recovery of all on-site costs from the beneficiaries.

The implementation of this market-oriented approach had led to serious delays and doubts some feel may lead to the ultimate abandonment of the ZIP approach. Between 1977 and 1980, only thirteen more project sites were planned for the period 1980–4.

7.4 Land tenure

Most students of self-help housing practices argue that only a low level of housing improvements can be expected unless people have 'reasonable' security of tenure of the land. Just what is a 'reasonably' secure tenure arrangement is less clear, as a recent empirical assessment of international experience has demonstrated (Angel 1980).

The tenure question was approached differently in the four cities, reflecting both the political and administrative difficulties associated with the transfer and registration of freehold types of title to previously illegal (or unregistered) low-income residents. The KIP in Jakarta has bypassed the issue of tenure as a matter of policy. Given the complicated traditional tenure arrangements and the miniscule, highly fragmented, and unrecorded holding of (urban) land properties, it was not feasible to clarify and register land rights at the speed with which the programme covered the various kampong areas. Although technically all kampong developments were illegal after 1945 and some kampong areas were developed on abandoned Dutch property, the programme ultimately included these areas as well. The only important tenure security statement enunciated in the policy covered the length of the assured period within which the improved area will remain undisturbed by redevelopment projects. This is to be five years. In practical terms, such an assurance is largely meaningless; the sheer size of the urban area covered by the programme is just too big to expect large-scale pressures for 'gentrification' or redevelopment. But those strategically situated kampongs, mostly in the city centre, which could be the target for redevelopment by commercial interests will have little chance of remaining, whether improved or not, given the evident sympathy of Jakarta's urban planners for a 'modern' urban landscape.

In contrast with the KIP's *laissez-faire* attitude towards the tenure issue, the settlement improvement programme in Papua New Guinea treats security of tenure as one of its core components. During the improvement process, a settlement and the land area around it is re-designed into an organized subdivision in which each settler is awarded a long lease on a plot of his or her own. Such a lease arrangement is common practice on all government land in Papua New Guinea, and so the upgrading process does not create a distinctly separate land market or administrative arrangement. In fact, the faithful imitation of existing subdivision practices (standards, surveying and marketing) has been criticized as an unnecessary administrative procedure delaying the programme's implementation and increasing its overhead costs.

The tenure issue is also central to the ZIP policy in the Philippines, partly because of the bitter experience of arbitrary resettlement practices carried out under the previous policy and partly because of the importance that Filipinos attach to individual land ownership. However, the process of tenure legalization pioneered by the Tondo projects is complicated and likely to be inapplicable in dense, inner city ZIP sites. It involves 'tagging' structures and registering the resident population, which is supposed to freeze development in the area. The next step is to propose three alternatives for 'reblocking' the area, all of which involve some resettlement of residents and structures to adjoining sites and services projects. Reblocking implies the subdivision of both private plots and public rights of way. Those awarded a plot within the existing area receive a twenty-five year transferable lease which includes the option to purchase a freehold title. Those who move to a sites and services plot can acquire tenure on similar conditions.

In preparing the slum upgrading policy for Bangkok, the NHA also developed an elaborate mechanism of ensuring security of tenure for residents in improved neighbourhoods as well as a degree of protection from arbitrary rent increases. The proposed mechanism was the transfer of land from public or institutional owners to the NHA in the form of long-term leases which would, in turn, be sublet by NHA to the residents. The slum upgrading office also worked out various methods of acquiring individual houses not inhabited by the owners, and selling or leasing them to their tenants. Long-term agreements between landowners and current tenants were proposed (with five-year, controlled rent increases) when upgrading was implemented on private property. While the policy-makers at the NHA were clearly concerned with the tenure implications of the upgrading programme, they failed to anticipate the political limits of government intervention in the land market or the bureaucratic implications of administering the multitude of lease arrangements and fee collections. As a result, the NHA now merely seeks permission from both private and public or institutional landowners to enter the property and improve basic infrastructure without obtaining any formal commitment from the landlord to grant long-term security to the tenants. Ironically while new legal instruments have been proposed by the NHA to provide the authority with greater legislative power to force landowners to accept slum improvement with security of tenure, the same officials are now worrying that such an intervention may have the effect of drying up the (unserviced) land supply for low-income families (Sidhijai 1980: 191).

7.5 Infrastructure standards

With the extension of municipal services to popular housing areas the question arises as to what level of standard is to be applied. The issue is resolved by the adjustment of political, economic, engineering and practical considerations. At the political level, the minimum service standard must be compatible with government retaining a degree of credibility, in that citizens see a marked improvement in conditions. The average service levels pertaining in the city aid the citizens (the political constituency) in deciding whether the standards applied to the upgrading programme are too high or too low. As no government can escape the economic costs of service provision, the level of services will also be influenced by the budgetary constraints of the programme. Thus within these constraints, a choice must be made between increasing the scale of the programme, at the expense of the level of services or offering less coverage, with higher (and therefore more visible) standards. The engineering and technical considerations usually address the issue of service standards from the point of view of their performance and long-term maintenance implications. Engineers would argue that the design specifications of some infrastructure components (especially water supply, drainage, and waste disposal systems) are so low that they will either fail to achieve the expected output or their performance will rapidly deteriorate due to their inadequate material strength or maintenance. Finally, the shape, density, types of structures and soil conditions of the present low-income settlement will define the practical limits of service standards. For the implementation of different types and standards of services will have different implications for the maintenance of the existing layout of the settlement and the amount of (internal and external) relocation that the proposed improvement will require.

The lowest level of services are indeed found in the KIP programme in Indonesia, which concentrates on the provision of road and walkway construction, some drainage, limited water supply and community toilets and washing places. Given the extremely low level of services in Jakarta as a whole (in 1968, only 27 per cent of houses had individual water connections, 5 per cent had treated sewerage, and 34 per cent had access to vehicular roads), this minimum service level was politically acceptable, and even considered generous. That the municipal government could raise only a meagre budget locally (US $17 *per capita*) was a compelling reason for keeping service provision at a low standard if the programme was to cover a significant area in the city. The high density of inner city kampongs and permanent houses and the fact that land for infrastructure was donated by the communities provided the practical

limitations on adjusting standards to a level which did not require extensive demolition and resettlement. While engineers and technicians
warned (correctly, as it turned out) that the material standards used for
infrastructure work were too low, their advice was eventually overruled
by the other considerations. Over the years, the KIP's standards have
been increased as new budget support was provided by the IBRD loan
and moderate density kampongs became the targets for improvement.

The standards applied in the NHA's slum improvement programme
in Bangkok also emphasize a low-cost and minimum displacement approach. Here the practical constraints are similar to those in Indonesia:
high existing densities, difficulty of moving structures and lack of
available land, except for what the community (or landowner) is willing
to concede. The much higher average service distribution in the city (87
per cent of slum residents have access to piped water, and almost all
houses have electricity connections) enables the NHA to concentrate on
selected service elements such as drainage, access, waste collection and
fire protection. Higher budgetary commitments (US $43 *per capita*) and
a much slower speed of implementation have made it possible for the
NHA to design service components of a better material quality than in
Jakarta. Neither the NHA programme or KIP worried about houses.

The general orientation of the settlement improvement policy in
Papua New Guinea is to create a framework for self-help housing construction which has comparable standards to the rest of the 'official' city.
The reorganization of settlements into new subdivisions is possible
because (a) the existing houses can be easily dismantled, (b) cheap,
government-owned land is available in adjacent areas, and (c) the
programme operates with a budget ($250 *per capita*) proportionately
higher than the other programmes in South East Asia. The generally
high service provision in Port Moresby (practically all households, outside of migrant settlements, have access to paved roads, piped water,
waste disposal and electricity) also represented an important existing
yardstick from which it was politically difficult to deviate substantially.
Thus the service element in the improvement of migrant settlements
includes paved vehicle roads and footpaths, individual water and
electricity connections, pit latrines and garbage collection. Given the
prolonged history of technicians pressing for high standards, ironically it
is the group of professionals now working with the migrant settlement
improvement programme who are pressing for the reduction of service
standards for the city as a whole, because they have realized the long-
term financial implications of maintaining existing norms when urban
immigration becomes strong in the future.

Service standards for the ZIP in Manila are also relatively high, reflecting the government's political objective of demonstrating that slum communities can be integrated into the modern image of the metropolitan city. The range of services includes road and footpath access, individual water connection, sanitary toilets and sewerage, drainage, street lighting and individual electricity connection (on demand) at a cost level of $188 per capita. The incorporation of such a high service level requires some reorganization of the existing physical layout of communities. This is facilitated by the fact that most homes can be moved without necessarily dismantling them.

7.6 Cost recovery

The strategy of financing settlement improvement programmes must resolve a number of different issues:

1 Can we expect the residents of low-income settlements to pay for the services and assets they receive through these projects? When the community is composed of a mixed income group, say those falling within the lowest 5–50 per cent range, would such a requirement push out the poorest, leading to further income segregation in the housing market?
2 Municipal services are usually routinely provided as part of local government responsibility, and financed from user charges and property and excise taxes at the local government level or budgetary transfers from the central government. When the settlement improvement programme breaks these components down into 'project packages' they appear as capital costs chargeable to local residents. Is this going to be acceptable?
3 When families receive freehold or leasehold title to property as part of the tenure regularization programme they acquire an asset in the urban land market. What should be the transfer price: the current market value of adjacent ('officially' developed) properties, a deflated price of the squatted property reflecting the fact that its use is fixed and practically unmarketable, or the likely market price of the upgraded plots? Or are these questions largely academic in the light of the organized refusal of the communities to pay for the land at all?
4 How to obtain capital necessary to start the settlement improvement programme, or to continue it when the recovery of costs is not linked to the actual beneficiaries.

The programmes in Jakarta, Bangkok, Manila and Papua New Guinea embody different approaches to these issues and offer some inconclusive experiences.

To take the last issue first, there appears to be a heavy reliance on outside loans to pursue settlement programmes on a metropolitan or national scale. While the KIP in Jakarta started as a local government initiative, its rapid enlargement to cover the whole city over a reasonable period of time and its extension to other Indonesian cities required external assistance from the IBRD and other bilateral sources. The IBRD also supplemented the budget of the slum improvement programmes in Bangkok and Manila, support which now takes the form of a series of urban sector lending arrangements. Yet, placed within the context of municipal budgets the infrastructure service development components of settlement improvement programmes are relatively minor expenditures. For Jakarta, KIP-related expenditures take up about 18 per cent of the yearly development budget of the city. In Bangkok, infrastructure costs of the slum improvement programme account for 2 per cent of the yearly capital expenditure of seven key public agencies associated with urban development and servicing functions in the Bangkok metropolitan region. And in the Philippines, the implementation of the ZIP without direct cost recovery from residents would consume about 4 per cent of the combined services budgets of the cities and municipalities which form Metro-Manila.

Thus affordability on the local government level should not be a major constraint on settlement improvement strategies, although these aggregate percentage figures hide a number of difficulties which need to be resolved before upgrading programmes can be viewed as a routine municipal responsibility. On the one hand, the local government budgets referred to above have a substantial central government resource transfer component. The inability to finance urban service development from property taxation and user charges alone is a common problem facing cities all over the world, but the imbalance between locally raised revenues and budget grants from higher levels of government is acute in developing countries (Smith 1974). The fact that central government transfers are often tied (in that they are accompanied by explicit instructions as to what types of project they can be used for, and the standards, accounting and decision-making practices to be followed) allows local authorities little flexibility in responding to local problems.

On the other hand, local government decision-making in the past has often favoured higher income groups and prestigious projects when disposing of the budget that was under its control. Indeed it did not have much alternative. The urban economy which has generated the wealth of the high-income élite achieved this accumulation process through both urban and rural pauperization. The urban environment which resulted from the individual investment of what poor urban families could afford to spend generated extremely low-quality neighbourhoods with practically no residential services, while local governments had to develop and sustain infrastructure components for the modern industrial sector, the administrative and commercial centres, high-income residential areas and for a convenient road network linking the segregated urban sectors. It appears that when this vicious cycle of capitalist urban development based on the socialization of the generation of wealth through low wages and the socialization of the cost of high environmental quality development through public spending threatens the overall viability of the social system, it is the central government which steps in with additional funding to service low-income housing areas.

Given these contradictions, the low percentage of the overall municipal budget allocated for the provision of infrastructure components of upgrading projects and the history of neglect in past municipal service performance, the strategy of direct cost recovery of public investment from the residents of low-income settlements remains politically unfeasible in two of the cities. In Jakarta, the KIP policy was initially formulated as a regular government infrastructure service, for which long-term finance would be generated through improved administration of existing land taxation and higher rates for land on which specialized commercial activities were located. In Bangkok, the original policy proposed a degree of direct cost recovery for infrastructure work incorporated into the new lease prices. However, when it became evident that no tenure regularization was feasible, the concept of direct cost recovery of capital expenditure was also dropped.

Incorporating the migrant settlement improvement programme into the reoriented self-help housing strategy of the national government in Papua New Guinea implied that all low-income housing projects would operate under the normal system of recovery mechanisms. This excludes raw land costs but includes on-site development costs which are passed on to the residents as yearly plot charges in the form of lease arrangements. However, the high rates of delinquency in paying the lease fee indicates that people either could not afford the burden of financing the full cost of the infrastructure provision or simply refused to take responsibility for it.

It is proposed that both on-site infrastructure development costs and the price of land acquisition will be recovered from the direct beneficiaries of the upgraded settlements in Manila. This recovery arrangement appears to be acceptable to the residents of the first projects in Tondo and payments are now being collected. However, whether people will regularly pay over a period of twenty-five years remains to be seen. While the good start made by Tondo residents is taken as an encouraging sign by the NHA technical team, the transferability of this experience to other ZIP sites is less certain. In the first place, the land price component in Tondo was very low, reflecting the collective strength of the community when a price was first established during negotiations with the government in 1955. In other ZIP sites, the residents are scheduled to pay a land transfer cost which is only marginally lower than current market prices. The second difference is the complicated internal sub-letting and renting arrangements that prevail in some of the inner city ZIP areas. The allocation of costs to individual families will require a degree of sophistication and arbitrariness which will certainly lead to many disagreements among the residents.

The transfer of tenure rights as an asset in the urban land market has occurred in only two of the cities – Port Moresby and Manila. In Papua New Guinea, families receive the plot with a long-term lease from the government, but ownership remains with the state. Consequently families do not pay the capital price of the land but merely nominal user charges. The land rent fee is independent of location and site conditions, and varies only according to the size of the plot.

The presidential decree which established the ZIP in the Philippines gave the implementing agency a powerful legal tool to acquire the land on which the squatter communities are located and ultimately to transfer the improved plots to the residents either on an ownership or leasehold basis. The decree provides a quick procedural mechanism for the NHA to start the upgrading work before final agreement on the purchase of the property is negotiated. However, the economic mechanism which guides the process of transferring the near-market cost of the acquired property to the beneficiaries is less clear. Given the substantial differences in land prices on ZIP sites (ranging from 206 pesos, or approximately \$25 at 1982 exchange rates, to 5 pesos/m^2) some communities simply could not afford to pay for the land transfer cost. To overcome this problem, the NHA proposes to create a mechanism of cross subsidy by averaging out land acquisition costs among the sites. However, this proposal has not been implemented yet and therefore there is no empirical evidence available to judge whether it is workable, that is, whether residents on land worth 5 pesos/m^2 will pay 50 pesos for it.

7.7 Upgrading projects v. improvement programmes

Since the early 1960s international agencies and a growing group of professionals and academics have advocated a positive policy towards those low-income settlements which have evolved outside the legal framework of urban planning in developing countries. As recommended, the core of such a policy should be a form of tenure security, the extension of public services and a degree of direct cost recovery to sustain the improvement for a large number of settlements over a long time period.[5] Today these recommendations have been translated into a series of settlement improvement projects in the large cities of South East Asia with various degrees of success. In Thailand, the Philippines and Papua New Guinea the implementing agencies are central government bodies who in the past had some experience with low-cost housing projects, but played only a marginal role in the practice of urban development. In Indonesia, though central government also plays an important co-ordinating role, partly because of its financial obligation towards IBRD, the implementation of settlement improvement is largely left to the municipal authorities.

The experiences in these countries demonstrate that the simultaneous implementation of tenure transfer, residential service provision and direct cost recovery as a single project package is difficult to achieve. Jakarta and Bangkok provide evidence that urban governments can afford public service provisions at low and medium levels of standards without direct charges for the development cost (as opposed to user charges related to operating costs) and can expand such a programme quickly. This may or may not lead to the physical improvement of the houses, but can certainly improve health conditions in the settlement as well as providing more than a symbolic gesture for the urban poor that they are legitimate urban citizens. Once the programme links the provision of infrastructure with the tenure transfer of individual plots, progress can be expected to be slow and become selective, as the implementation of ZIP in Manila suggests. Whether it ultimately leads to the further marginalization of the poorest families in the neighbourhood is too early to say. Cost recovery from the residents will perhaps remain an elusive goal unless costs are reduced substantially and perceived by the community as socially just. Current preoccupation with dubious calculations whether the charges are 'affordable' are clearly not very useful.

There appears to be a fairly strong concern among residents of low-income settlements as to what they should pay for. These are connection and user charges for individual services and land title transfer costs representing the price of land at the time of occupation. They do not wish to pay 'development' costs for infrastructure and current market costs for land whether these combined charges are skilfully assessed for their 'affordability' or not.

When settlement improvement is framed as a series of projects with its budgeted cost components, including land acquisition cost from the private owner or opportunity cost for public land, the gap between what the beneficiaries are willing to pay and the needed revenue to sustain similar projects is indeed wide. However if the public works component of settlement improvement is cast within the budgetary practice of urban development, the arguments for direct cost recovery appear in a different light. It is the city, its total population, its industrial and commercial enterprises which should share the cost of the overall evolution of infrastructure services rather than those communities which have long been excluded in the past. If today these services are run on deficits, they do so because those who already have the services were never asked to pay for full cost recovery. The 'project package' thus side-steps the issue of appraising broader financial reform for urban management.

Similarly, the attempted practice to incorporate the current or close to the current market price of land into the transfer payment for individual plot owners has failed to gain community acceptance. Among the case studies here, only ZIP projects in the Philippines implemented land transfer, and the government had to settle for a plot price which the residents demanded. With this precedent, the projects are locked into a continuous confrontation in all other sites in Manila, where residents demand equal treatment. Thus the alternative is that the government subsidizes the difference between the market cost at which it acquires land and the disposal cost at which it transfers the property to local residents. This approach contains an insoluble contradiction, in that the government will never have a budget capable of extending the programme beyond a few show-cases.

7.8 Conclusions

In concluding it may also be useful to discuss whether the practice of improving existing low-income settlements has changed official attitudes toward ones in formation. For in each city the initial surveys and feasibility studies found that most of the housing areas which in the past were excluded from public services because of their illegal status are in fact suitable residential locations, and could offer a low-quality but safe and decent living environment, once improved. Therefore, it may be possible to move from the concept of an evolutionary housing development strategy to that of an evolutionary settlement development strategy.

Of the four case studies, Indonesia comes nearest to this perspective. While not encouraged, kampong formation is still an accepted practice of housing development, and the KIP is programmed to continue to improve newly formed or expanding kampongs indefinitely. In Bangkok, the official attitude is more ambiguous. While not explicitly stating that newly formed slum areas will not be improved, the large number of existing settlements already selected for improvement and the relatively slow rate of implementation makes their incorporation only a distant possibility. However, the argument put forward privately by some officials involved with the slum upgrading programme is that a too radical move towards tenure security in upgraded slums could damage the existing balance of the low-income housing market, particularly the rental prices being paid (Sidhijai 1980) and this does imply an acceptance of slum formation as a legitimate or necessary development model. In Papua New Guinea, the provision of an excess supply of building plots in and around improved migrant settlements aims to prevent the spontaneous creation of new ones. Whether the authorities will be able to develop a sufficient supply can only be judged in a few years' time. The current preoccupation in Port Moresby is to find solutions to the spontaneous development of settlements on customary land which is now beyond the control of the municipal administration (Forster 1979: 378).

Ironically, while the ZIP programme in the Philippines includes a most comprehensive set of project components for low-income settlement improvement, it also takes the most hostile attitude towards families who may in the future develop housing solutions similar to those which are now being improved. This hostility is not confined to future developments alone. The presidential order, enacted in 1977, initiating the ZIP, also froze existing settlements and took a census of their inhabitants; no area developed after this date is eligible for improvement. Thus slum upgrading is seen in the Philippines as a limited corrective measure for what happened in the 1950s and 1960s rather than as continuous public participation in the people's housing effort.

In summary, then, the experience of the four countries shows that indigenous, historically conditioned land markets, political institutions, and the contemporary political climate shape settlement improvement programmes and determine their workings far more than do the current international models of upgrading and self-help housing.

Notes

1 In the Asian context the following examples offer an illustration:

   i In Madras, India, the Tamil Nadu Slum Clearance Board was established in 1970 with the task of rehousing the city's slum population, estimated to be 221,000 families, in public tenements within seven years. By 1977, however, the Board was able to construct only 32,000 units. At that time the programme was abandoned in favour of on-site improvement (Ambados 1979: 9).

ii In Thailand the National Housing Authority scrapped its public housing construction targets (largely set to build 'low-cost' multi-storey dwellings for low- and middle-income groups) in 1978 and embarked on a 'sites and services' and 'slum improvement' programme instead (Chawalit Nitaya 1979: 5).

iii In Papua New Guinea the government abandoned any form of public housing construction in favour of a 'self-help' approach in 1975 (Papua New Guinea 1975).

iv In Indonesia the housing targets set out for the government housing agency do not cover more than a modest 15 per cent of the projected urban housing needs. This target, however, was only 80 per cent achieved in the first five-year plan. On the other hand, Singapore and Hong Kong are often cited as examples for the feasibility of vigorous public housing construction programmes. For a broader analysis of the affordability of public sector housing by low-income groups in developing countries, see Grimes (1976: 63–81).

2 It is difficult to provide comparative data on the new housing stock developed by agents of the 'informal' housing market. In most countries statistics focus exclusively on the growth of squatter areas which by no means exhaust the range of popular action in housing. In some others 'slum' areas are also included which, in fact, represent a more intensive use and the subsequent deterioration of existing houses. The diversity of forms which popular housing may take in a number of Asian cities is summarized by Angel *et al.* (1977).

3 Rodell (1980a) presents the potential advantages of 'evolutionary strategies' as:

i a reduction in construction costs for many low-income families by providing land more suitable for residential development than where squatters are currently located;

ii specializing government inputs into land and infrastructure development which agencies can handle more efficiently than the supervision of house construction;

iii spreading government resources over more families;

iv a substantial improvement in health conditions due to the provision of piped water, garbage collection and drainage;

v the mobilization of resources, especially labour at the family level, which otherwise are not used in conventional housing strategies.

4 A similar argument is developed by Crooke *et al.* (1977) in reviewing the squatter and slum formation process in some fifteen cities in Africa, Asia and Latin America.

5 At the rhetorical level local participation in decision-making and socio-economic development programmes were also among such recommendations, without any serious analysis of the feasibility of either having been made.

References

Ambados, A. (1979) 'Case study on improving low income residential areas at Madras – Tamil Nadu (India)', paper presented to Seminar on Improving Low Income Residential Areas in South East Asian Cities, Bandung, Indonesia, 29 October to 17 November.

Angel, S. (1980) *Land Tenure for the Urban Poor*, Bangkok, Asian Institute of Technology, Human Settlements Division, Working Paper 1.

Angel, S., Benjamin, S., and De Goede, K. (1977) 'The low-income housing system in Bangkok', *Ekistics*, 261, August, 78–84.

Baross, P. (1980) 'Analysis of housing production systems. Bandung, Indonesia', *Open House* (4), 3, 44–61.

Chawalit Nitaya (1979) *Tung Song Hong: Community Involvement, an Alternative Design and Policy Implementation Proposal*, Rotterdam, Institute for Housing Studies Bulletin RS1.

Crooke, P., Sarin, M., Payne, G., McNeill, D., McDonald, I. and Winpenny, J. (1977) 'Urban housing review', London, University of London, Development Planning Unit, 3 vols, mimeo.

Devas, N. (1980) 'Indonesia's kampong improvement programme. An evaluation case study', Birmingham, UK, University of Birmingham, Development Administration Group, mimeo.

Forster, B. (1979) 'Some urbanization problems in a developing Papua New Guinea', *Ekistics*, 279, November–December, 378–81.

Grimes, O. (1976) *Housing for Low-Income Urban Families*, Baltimore and London, Johns Hopkins University Press.

Koenigsberger, O. (1974) lecture series, London, University of London, Development Planning Unit.

Norwood, H. (1979) 'Port Moresby: pattern of settlement among migrants and urban villagers (National Capital District)', in C. and B. Valentine (eds) *Going through Changes: Villagers, Settlers and Development in Papua New Guinea*, Port Moresby, Institute of Papua New Guinea Studies, pp. 72–89.

Papua New Guinea (1975) *National Housing Plan, Part One*, Port Moresby, Ministry of the Interior, Housing Commission.

Philippines (1975) *Pahra '75*, Manila, Presidential Assistant on Housing and Resettlement Agency, Terminal Report, October.

Rodell, M. (1980a) 'Low-income housing strategies: a discussion paper', Rotterdam, Institute for Housing Studies, March, mimeo.

Rodell, M. (1980b) 'Colombo, Sri Lanka', in M. Sarin (ed.) *Policies towards Urban Slums. Slums and Squatter Settlements in the ESCAP Region*, Bangkok, United Nations, ESCAP.

Sidhijai Tanphiphat (1980) 'Security of land tenure for slum upgrading: a case study in Bangkok', in *Human Settlements in the Development Process*, vol. 1 of the proceedings of the 7th EAROPH Congress, Kuala Lumpur, Malaysian Organization for Human Settlements, pp. 180–94.

Smith, R. (1974) 'Financing cities in developing countries', *International Monetary Fund Staff Papers*, 21 (2), July, 329–89.

Turner, J. (1976) *Housing by People*, London, Marion Boyars.

8
Popular housing supports and the urban housing market

P. CROOKE

8.1 Introduction

This chapter describes some of the ways in which governmental supports for popular housing, undertaken during the past two decades largely as emergency measures under the pressures of unplanned urban growth, have also begun to establish new and interdependent roles for formal and informal housing organizations and resources — roles that can lead to radically new opportunities in the housing sector if we can make positive use of the experience gained so far in supporting popular housing through sites and services (SS) and slum upgrading (SU) programmes.

Meanwhile there are some clear indications in many Third World countries that the ways in which governments are providing supports for popular housing create new and valuable prizes for the housing market as a whole — where eventual benefit still ends up in the hands of the highest bidder. Can governmental supports for popular housing develop in ways which make use of the undoubted efficiencies of the housing market without merely providing, in the long term, further opportunities for this market to exploit the urban poor?

To look at this question in any more detail we need to recognize some important innovations that SS and SU work has been bringing to the urban housing market in Third World countries in the last two decades. We need also to recognize some factors limiting the extent to which work of this kind benefits the urban poor, and contributes to institutional changes in the land and housing markets that confront them.

8.2 Innovations in supporting popular housing

What are the main innovations that SS and SU work is bringing with it? Firstly, it entails a new way of organizing the various goods and services that make land habitable: land areas and boundaries; infrastructure works for road and foot access; water supply, drainage and sanitation; residential services such as schools, clinics, markets and recreation areas and, of course, houses themselves.

In the conventional development of new housing we are accustomed to the idea that all these goods and services need to be brought into use as nearly simultaneously as possible in a single 'package': a housing project in which each dwelling has its prearranged share of housing land, its connections to access and utilities networks of all kinds, and its share in the use of schools and other residential services. But the upgrading needs of any popular housing area, for example, make the rationale of this conventional housing package irrelevant: people are already making full use of the area's dwellings long before enjoying the use of most residential utilities and services, and often without legal entitlement to the land they occupy. Moreover, the shortage of money for paying the area's upgrading costs makes necessary a discussion and choice of priorities among the housing goods and services available, and a development programme by which these can be attained over a relatively long period of time; in fact, the exact opposite of an instant housing package.

In other words, the incremental improvement of an existing area of popular housing 'explodes' the conventional housing package into an array of component options, each with its relevance or irrelevance to particular local conditions, and each attainable, over time, by combinations of inputs from households, local communities and local and national government.

Compared to upgrading, the early stages of development of land in SS work usually follow a more predictable and plannable course. But here also the same financial constraints apply and the same need for inputs over a long period from as wide as possible an array of contributors. During this process all the normal goods and services of the conventional housing package may eventually be achieved, but in an open-ended and loosely constructed way that can make use of the inputs of all these actors.

Various consequences stem from this 'explosion' or disaggregation of the conventional housing package, and they tend to make SS and SU work an effective support for popular housing practices. The open-ended investment period entailed in SS and SU work, and its practice of bringing residential land into use (and of legalizing the use of existing settlement land) long before it is fully developed, mean that both services and dwellings progress incrementally, in a gradual evolution from low standards and costs to higher ones. The gradual building and improving of one's house over time is of course already familiar to low-income householders in Third World towns and cities as a necessary strategy for attaining higher housing standards in urban conditions where all housing goods and services cost money. But for urban planning and housing authorities the toleration of cheap standards of land development and housing – even as a starting point in the development of a settlement – often runs counter to what their own backgrounds and training tell them they should be doing – enforcing and maintaining high and fixed standards of urban development and housing.

SS and SU work is beginning to provide the setting in which these rigid (and often unattainable) standards governing a settlement's physical form and cost are being superseded by more limited rules for the settlement's performance, ensuring that the public's health and safety are protected even at extremely low-cost and 'low-standard' stages in the settlement's development.

Another important contribution that SS and SU work has started to make to Third World urban development in the past decade or more, has been in establishing the notion that even planned and serviced urban development can be a self-financing operation. There are two main ways in which this notion has gained ground in SS and SU work in recent years. Firstly, through the recognition that if those investing public funds in urban land development and servicing keep their initial development standards and costs low, even low-income households can often afford to pay these costs back over time and still finance their own house-building and improvement. Secondly, by providing in SS work a variety of land and servicing standards and costs – for a wider range of households than those with low incomes alone, and for industrial and commercial as well as residential uses of land in a given settlement – public agencies are increasingly using surplus revenues from their higher-value provisions to subsidize the costs of plots and services for the poor. This can improve access by the poor to cheap and legal settlement land and services without requiring that these be subsidized from scarce public funds.[1]

In fact, the direct recovery of low development costs from the poor, and the cross-subsidization of these costs both from wealthier households and from income-generating uses of land, can make planned and serviced urban development very largely self-financing over time even when it may need quite large initial capital investment from the public sector. This recovery of costs can be crucial, as it can make the development of urban land and services for low-income use much more viable than has commonly been assumed in the past. Moreover, in the longer term, this improved use of local and national capital in revenue-generating urban development may gradually reduce Third World countries' need for international and other foreign capital in the urban development sector, and strengthen local and national independence in formulating urban development policies and programmes.

A mix of incomes (among SS residents in particular) and of industrial and commercial land uses in a given settlement can thus make a direct contribution to the recovery of its development costs. But SS and SU work is showing that benefits of another kind can also stem from the mixed development of urban land. SS work which caters for households with a relatively wide range of incomes changes a very common trend in all conventionally-supplied housing projects – the segregation of housing users by income and by social class and the relegation of low-income users to areas of 'mutual poverty' that further restrict their social and economic opportunities. Moreover, in both SS and SU work, planned provisions for local industries and commerce as income-generating parts of a settlement also allow a varied and productive use of settlement land, and a richer local environment than houses alone can provide.

In the long term, though, perhaps the most significant feature of SS and SU work will prove to be the new working relationships that it establishes between governmental bodies and the public at large, in the settlement and housing sector. We can see the beginnings of these new relationships at work in, for example, the upgrading of a settlement that has developed hitherto outside the law, with no external support.

Studies and consultations with the residents will identify certain parts of the upgrading programme that clearly need public sector intervention, and some that may need public sector funds as well; among these may be the legalization of land occupancy in the settlement, the introduction of basic services and the provision of loan finance for local businesses. But these actions (if successful) will spark off many later inputs – some of them perhaps needing external advice but none of them necessarily needing government control or management; for instance the upkeep and maintenance of community services, and the consolidation and improvement of the settlement's housing stock. These are matters that local community councils, local entrepreneurs and households themselves can usually manage and control far more effectively than can any government agency acting on their behalf. If SS and SU work continues to develop along these participatory lines, its role in strengthening and supporting grass roots organizations and leadership in popular urban settlements may take on a significance reaching far beyond the settlement and housing sector itself (Turner 1976: ch. 8).

One can sum this up by saying that SS and SU work is introducing important new features to the urban housing market in Third World countries. Among these is the work's basis in an array of housing goods and services – settlement land, road and utility networks, local facilities and dwellings – that can be developed in a variety of cost-recoverable combinations and sequences over time to meet the evolving needs of particular groups in the urban population. Essential to these actions is the way in which SS and SU work is bringing these goods and services into use: it provides for the first time the basis for a working collaboration between the resources of formal governmental and commercial institutions, and the informal resources of the low-income public at large (whose housing activities have in the past been largely ignored or frustrated).

8.3 Limitations and problems in popular housing support

It is also true, of course, that the potential importance of these features has not yet been fully realized: several factors still limit their impact in the urban settlement and housing sector. First among these factors is the relatively small scale so far of SS and SU work in relation to the massive and growing demand for urban settlement and housing opportunities. Work of this kind is being undertaken in an increasingly large number of countries, and in many of them, the objectives of SS and SU work (developed initially in local pilot projects) are now being embodied in national scale policies and programmes of support for popular housing. But even so, work of this kind in all but a very few Third World countries, has so far involved and affected only a tiny proportion of their low-income urban populations.

One can illustrate this by recalling that the World Bank (by far the largest single promoter and funder of SS and SU work until now) has estimated that some 10 million people benefited from its projects in the six years from 1974 to 1979 – up to 2 million people annually (Churchill 1979: 3). This compares with a current annual increase in the urban population of Third World countries as a whole of probably 40–50 million people (United Nations 1969: table 36) – with of course an enormously larger number already living in deficient housing conditions and receiving no support for their housing needs and actions.

Moreover even in those few countries where a substantial amount of SU and SS work has been undertaken, it is still too early to assess all its long-run effects. As we will see, there are signs that some of these bring disadvantages as well as advantages to the urban poor.

One problem is that both SS and SU work usually brings the activities of low-income residents under stricter external control both in their payments for urban services, and in their enterprises. Informally organized settlements support the poor not only by offering low-cost housing opportunities, but also by allowing irregular payment of rent and repayments of locally borrowed housing credit. The SS and SU work of official agencies usually increases the costs and payments above those that low-income residents would otherwise have to bear. It often imposes on poor families demands for higher housing standards and a regular payment discipline alien to their normal transactions, and especially difficult for those with irregular incomes.

At the same time, increased official control may reduce residents' income opportunities in a multitude of unregistered and untaxed local enterprises that would otherwise flourish in the area – another possible loss to the poor when SS and SU work 'co-opts' them into formal city arrangements for settlement and employment as junior members. One may ponder whether these gains in official control over a town or city's flourishing but irregular housing and business activities are an undeclared aim of many government-sponsored SS and SU projects.

Another reason for the questionable impact, so far, of SS and SU work can be found in the ways in which governmental authorities are undertaking work of this kind. In SS and SU work, funds are mostly being used for individual projects in which particular settlements or land areas are selected for treatment, often by project agencies created for this one purpose. To ensure the project's success, the agency is often provided with special funding and staffing advantages, and often exempted from building and planning regulations in force elsewhere in the city and the country.

These project conditions tend to isolate SS and SU work from the financial, manpower and bureaucratic problems confronting the rest of the country's public sector. As a result, there is relatively little spillover of SS and SU project experience beyond the project boundaries established for it. This limits its potential contribution in testing and demonstrating precedents for institutional reforms, for example, in the critical field of urban land ownership and tenure.

Indeed many of the current limitations of SS and SU work stem from the difficulty of introducing, in a circumscribed project area, settlement and housing innovations that run counter to the purposes and the workings of the surrounding land and housing market. There is already some evidence of how prevailing market forces are affecting the outcomes of SS and SU work, and in this chapter we look at examples of this in Thailand, the Philippines and Malawi.

8.4 Slum upgrading in Bangkok

In Thailand's capital, Bangkok, some 30 per cent of the city's population lives in slum settlements (World Bank 1980: 3), the majority of which are on privately owned lands. Development of the housing stock on these lands entails a variety of arrangements involving:

- landowners receiving land rent;
- intermediaries who pay this rent, and in turn either build and rent out rooms or houses or sublet parcels of land for residents' own house construction; and tenants who rent both the land and the house they occupy, or (less commonly) rent land on which they have built their own home.

Owner occupancy of both land and house is rare (Sidhijai 1980: 2ff.).

Bangkok's slums have been developed most densely on inner city land where grossly deficient urban services of all kinds have, until now, kept land and building rents low enough to be affordable by the urban poor. In Bangkok's current programme of slum upgrading, infrastructure improvements (mainly all-weather walkways, land drainage and water supplies) are being provided by the government, but the existing owner-ship of slum lands and buildings continues unchanged. The expropriation of slum lands would at present be politically feasible in Thailand only if land and building owners were compensated at full market value – a cost that neither the government nor the slum residents can possibly afford.

But the continuation of private ownership of these slum lands presents the problem that, if the slum's market value rises as a result of upgrading, the eventual benefits from this will accrue not to low-income slum residents (most of whom rent both house and land) but to higher-income owners of the slum's land and housing stock. Moreover there is a more immediate prospect: any rise in property values caused by upgrading will soon be reflected in rising land and house rents – a fine result for local property owners, but a disastrous one for many of their tenants.

To prevent this from happening, the Thai authorities intend to make the owners of upgraded slum areas and buildings undertake to keep rents at their present level in real terms, and to guarantee their tenants' security of tenure during the twenty years following upgrading. It would be hard enough to enforce such an undertaking in any case, but in Bangkok it is difficult for the authorities even to introduce them, since they need the landowner's permission before carrying out upgrading work on his land.

The tenure system also makes cost recovery difficult. It is held to be unfair to charge the tenants of slum land and housing with these costs; and in any case there is no practical way for the government to collect such payments from tenants, even if they were able and willing to pay them. Nor is it feasible to recover upgrading costs from slum land and building owners through the present, very leaky property tax system, and any attempt to charge owners in this or in other ways could be used by them as justification for raising their tenants' rents or refusing permission to upgrade. These difficulties have so far prevented the Thai authorities from attempting any direct recovery of slum upgrading costs, which are being financed from general governmental revenues and from World Bank loan capital (World Bank 1980: 37ff.).

These problems in upgrading privately owned slums, illustrated here by the Bangkok case, are to be found also in slums of Calcutta,[2] Jakarta and several other large cities of Asia where overcrowding and lack of land drainage, water supplies and sanitation make upgrading essential. There can be no doubt that slum tenants in all these cities are gaining immediate benefit from the improved infrastructure that upgrading brings, yet these improvements may be costing dear, in the loss of longer-term security, when they raise the market value of slum land and prompt its owners to raise rents, or to evict tenants and redevelop the land for more profitable uses.

8.5 Squatter settlement upgrading in Manila

In the Philippines, another Asian country with a 'free' market in urban land, upgrading of the Tondo squatter area of Manila is having some different consequences to those in Bangkok. The Tondo Foreshore is the largest single squatter settlement in the Philippines (plate 8.1). It has a population of about 180,000, and occupies some 445 acres (180 ha) of land adjacent to the city's port waterfront, where many Tondo residents work in the port and related industries (World Bank 1977: 2). This part of Manila was largely destroyed during the Second World War and was occupied by groups of homeless squatters during its post-war clearance and reclamation. Despite Tondo's location at Manila's centre, the illegality of its squatter housing and its lack of basic urban services combined to keep Tondo property values and rents low, and enabled low-paid city workers to build or rent accommodation there relatively cheaply.

During the post-war decades the unresolved campaigns and struggles of Tondo's population to obtain legal land titles and basic residential services became an increasingly sharp political issue in Manila (Poethig 1971: 123), and eventually led (in the later 1970s) to the provision of World Bank loan funds for upgrading most of the Tondo area, and for relocating a part of its population to allow for expansion of the port's facilities.

The upgrading programme in Tondo includes the provision of all-weather access, drainage and sewerage works, improved water supplies

Plate 8.1 Tondo foreshore area, Manila, Philippines.

and local facilities − and the provision of individual land titles to the owners of Tondo properties. These titles are nominally leaseholds paid for on a monthly basis, but their holders have the option of purchasing their titles outright after five years' tenure and of buying and selling them on the open market, so that in practice they enjoy most of the features of freehold land tenure.

Approximately one-half of Tondo's households, however, are tenants renting rooms or houses from those who are now becoming, for the first time, legal owners of Tondo property. The legalization of Tondo's housing stock, coupled with infrastructure improvements, is certainly providing the incentive for a high rate of local investment in improved housing. Now that Tondo is becoming a legal part of the city's housing market, however, its land titles and buildings are increasing rapidly in value with consequent increases in property sales to wealthier households, in rising rents and in the dislocation of low-income tenants of rented Tondo properties.

There is no doubt that, as in Bangkok's upgraded slums, all Tondo residents are gaining immediate benefit from its improved infrastructure, and that this and the provision of legal land titles are bestowing real financial gains to many owners of Tondo properties. But in the longer term, what will become of Tondo's present tenants as they are gradually squeezed out of this central area to make way for higher-value uses of Tondo land?

During the three post-war decades the range of social positions and incomes among Tondo households became more varied with the passing of time, and this was reflected in an increasingly wide range of housing standards and costs, and in the growing use of Tondo's housing stock for landlordism and rental as well as for home ownership. Yet during these decades of Tondo's illegality, both haves and have-nots, house owners and tenants among its residents, had in common the overriding need for self-defence – the need to fight eviction from the land and houses they were using. But the eventual legalization of Tondo's squatter land occupancy is benefiting Tondo owners at the expense of their tenants: market forces are, as it were, beginning to drive a 'financial wedge' between these two parts of what was previously a relatively united community.

We must, I think, question the basis of any upgrading work of this kind that strengthens the more regressive features of the urban property market, and provides physical improvements and financial gains in a way that promotes conflicts of interest within an existing urban community.

Thailand and the Philippines are among the Asian countries whose long histories of urban development have given them strongly established urban economies, and complex markets in urban property. In these conditions, land and building owners can, as we have seen, quickly make use of government-derived slum and squatter settlement improvements to further their own interests in the housing market.

8.6 Sites and services in Malawi

We can see a rather different picture in the countries of East, Central, and Southern Africa. Rural–urban migration and the growth of urban populations have of course increased enormously since the early 1960s, when political and economic changes following independence removed most restrictions on internal migration and began to provide more employment and career opportunities in urban centres. But this urbanization is generally taking place where the urban housing market has not developed along fully commercial lines.

These are countries where the use of land and housing as market commodities is still alien to the customs of most of their populations, and where the private ownership of land has been more a temporary device for legalizing land settlement and development by Europeans, than being the deeply rooted practice that it is in Asian and Latin American societies (United Nations 1975; World Bank 1978b: 188ff.).

In the absence of an active commercial market in urban land and housing, the initial development of low-income urban housing in these African countries has most commonly been in informal village-type settlements occupying communally held or state-owned lands around the urban centres. This has not generated any strong demand by settlers for individual land titles, or any large-scale private production of cheap urban housing for rental that one finds in Asia and Latin America. This common situation is now changing rapidly, however. The provision of housing sites and services in Malawi illustrates how this government action is providing raw material for the growth of a young and active urban housing market.

For the past fifteen years and more, public authorities in Malawi have been developing, in the country's larger towns, 'Traditional Housing Areas' – sites and services projects on peri-urban land subdivided into large house plots and equipped with basic access roads, communal water supplies, pit latrine sanitation and reservations for local facilities. These provisions have become a very important feature of the country's urban development: in Malawi's two largest centres, some 37 per cent of residents of Blantyre (1977 population 226,000) and some 51 per cent of residents of Lilongwe (1977 population 103,000) now live in SS areas, which are also being developed in several of the country's smaller towns. By 1981, some 27,000 plots had been developed in Malawi, housing more than a quarter of a million people, and during the 1970s, the provision of planned areas in Blantyre and Lilongwe very largely kept pace with the growth of these towns' low-income populations (Crooke 1981: 11–20).

This is a real achievement in a country that is urbanizing as fast as Malawi. Though nearly 90 per cent of the country's population still lives in rural areas, its urban population grew at an average rate of 8.5 per cent each year between 1966 and 1977 – one of the highest national rates in Africa (Malawi 1980). In Malawi, as in most countries of the region, there are large peri-urban areas of both communally held and state-owned lands that can be transferred to SS use at very low cost. In Malawi's schemes, the subdivisions of this land are leased to their holders, mostly on monthly tenure; there is no evidence that this short tenure is discouraging settlers from investing in housing of an affordable standard (mostly using mud brick walls and corrugated iron roofs), and housing in these areas is being developed quickly and without public sector funding.

A remarkable feature in Malawi's Traditional Housing Areas is the high and increasing proportion of rental housing they contain (figure 8.1). The house plots provided are large – 4000–5000 square feet (367–460 m²), and on them most settlers are building rental accommodation for at least

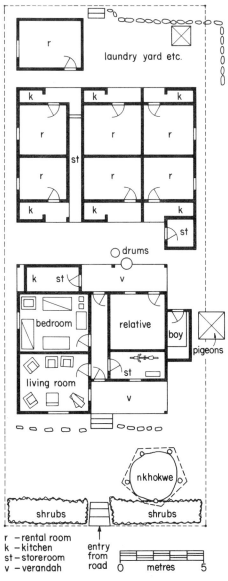

r — rental room
k — kitchen
st — storeroom
v — verandah

entry
from
road

0   metres   5

Figure 8.1 Malawi: Traditional Housing Area plot (12 × 30 m) showing plot holder's and tenants' accommodation.

Source: 3 April 1979 survey by M. Polela.

one or two tenant households, as well as housing for their own families. In Lilongwe 68 per cent of all residents belong to tenant households, and in Blantyre the tenant proportion is as high as 82 per cent in the city's longer-established SS areas (Centre for Social Research 1981; Malawi 1979).

In fact these areas are providing for a most important supply not only of owner-occupied housing, but also of rental accommodation for urban workers (with or without urban families) who have not yet obtained urban houses of their own. In Malawi, as in other countries of the region, many of these tenants are immigrants who still come to the country's towns and cities as short-term earners rather than as permanent urban settlers.

It is difficult to calculate accurately the income that rental housing is generating for the plot holders; but evidence suggests that the rents charged generally represent a 30–40 per cent annual return on the cost of room and house construction. In fact rents from tenants are commonly paying off, within little more than five years, not only the plot holder's costs in building his rental rooms but also the cost of building his own family's accommodation on the plot (Gondwe 1981: 7ff.).

This rental income is important not only because it means that Malawi's SS housing can quickly become self-financing (and indeed profitable), but also because it is providing many low-income plot holders with their sole means of accumulating capital in Malawi's urban economy, where jobs are scarce and wages are low. Whether this rental situation is also a good one for SS tenants, however, seems to depend very largely on the future rate of production of new plots. If SS development in Malawi continues to keep pace with the growth of urban population, at least in the country's larger towns, we can expect the supply of rental housing in these towns to grow fast enough to keep rents competitive and affordable. And this rate of SS development should also enable existing tenants as well as future urban newcomers to become plot holders and home owners themselves when this can benefit them.

8.7 The impact of market forces

The Malawi case illustrates how public sector action ensuring an adequate supply of certain housing resources (in this case, housing land and services) can help maintain an approximate balance between supply and demand in the low-income housing market − with benefits to house owners and tenants alike − while government relies on households themselves to raise and recover their own housing finance, and to manage their own housing activities. SS work, and SU work also, can certainly contribute positively to the urban housing market when settlement land is freely enough available to allow it to play this role.

The main reason why the upgrading in Bangkok and Manila seems likely to make things harder for most slum and squatter settlement tenants (by leading, among other things, to rising property values and rents) is that in these two cities the housing market flourishes not on a steady supply of cheap and legal housing land, but on its scarcity. And upgrading in these Asian cities is tending to worsen this scarcity by remedying slums' illegality, or lack of services, or both and thus increasing slums' potential for developments more profitable than cheap housing.

These consequences would be less severe, for slum tenants in particular, if public authorities in these cities were also bringing into use enough well-placed settlement land to provide slum tenants and other low-income households with viable alternative locations in the city, but this is not the case. Though SS schemes are being developed in both these cities, they are subject to the same market conditions of scarcity and high land value that already handicap the urban poor. For in Thailand and the Philippines the housing market is based upon the private ownership of land itself as a commodity with its own market value — and of course the greater the land demand, the higher its value and its price become.

When, in these market conditions, settlement land and services in SS projects are priced on a real-cost basis needed for cost recovery, they are usually in relatively convenient locations but are too expensive for low-income households to occupy; or they are relatively distant from the rest of the urban area, in 'fringe' or 'satellite' locations where the advantage of lower land prices is vitiated for low-income settlers by high travel costs to city work and amenities.

When, in the same market conditions, upgrading improvements raise land values in an existing settlement, this will of course benefit the owners of the upgraded area's land and the effects of this for the urban poor are more complex. Where these owners are mostly relatively wealthy landlords — as in Bangkok's slums — the eventual effect on low-income residents of the area is likely to be adverse in terms of their rental costs and their security. Where the owners of the upgraded land include low-income households, on the other hand — as in Manila's Tondo — any rise in the land's value following upgrading will, of course, benefit them. But in both these cases it seems likely that rising values and rents will make things more difficult for low-income tenants, whatever the income of the owner of the house they occupy.

There is no sign at present, in Thailand or the Philippines, that the authorities intend to use SS and SU work as part of any search for solutions to these problems posed by their urban land and housing markets (cf. Sidhijai 1980).

In Malawi, meanwhile, the large-scale supply of cheap urban land and services that feeds the low-income housing market is possible because, in that country, most peri-urban land is either held by a local community or owned by the state. In either case it cannot be privately bought or sold, and rights to its use can be transferred through government at very little cost, and without entailing ownership or purchase of the land itself by its users.

It could be argued however that in Malawi's sites and services we are merely witnessing early stages in the growth of market mechanisms that, starting with the present-day rental of property on SS plots, will come to include settlement land itself as a market commodity bought and sold among owners and accessible to the highest bidder. But this is not yet the case, and surely it need never happen as long as people continue confident that their rights to the use of land are assured. In Malawi, this confidence appears to be so strong that not even the extraordinarily brief monthly tenure entitlement to plots dispels it.

What lessons can we draw from these impacts of market forces on governments' supports for popular housing? One lesson seems to be that the legalizing and servicing of existing low-income settlements, in projects where these actions support or introduce private ownership of the settlement's land, will tend over time to price the settlement beyond the reach of low-income renters, even when these initially form a majority of the settlement's population.

A more general version of the same lesson is that the private ownership of urban land and the market mechanisms of supply and demand by which this ownership is transferred, tend over time to reduce the security of viable urban locations for the poor, in so far as they are obliged to conform to these market mechanisms.

Another lesson seems to be that people's residential security depends upon their enjoyment of rights to the use of settlement land, but not necessarily upon their owning it; and that in major parts of the Third World the very concept of land ownership is still alien, unfamiliar, and unnecessary.

8.8 Future developments in popular housing support

What can we do about lessons of this kind? Can we only expect sites and services and upgrading to relieve some immediate symptoms of housing stress, with the good and the bad consequences that we have looked at in this chapter? Or can we make it also introduce to the urban housing market some more fundamental changes of benefit to the urban poor?

In the mixed economies of most rapidly urbanizing countries, this more radical aim would require us to test and develop changes that both increase and maintain access by the poor to housing resources of all kinds and, most importantly, access to urban settlement land.

During the post-war decades of unprecedented demand by the poor for urban land, the most direct way that low-income groups have overcome the land market barriers confronting them has been to break the property laws, by invading and developing land to which they have no ownership rights. Squatting has often been effective and productive (Mangin 1967; Turner 1966), but it offers no stable institutional answer to problems of land ownership and high urban land prices.

Can we use sites and services and upgrading as a local means of developing institutional changes in the urban land market, and of testing alternatives to individual private ownership for, at least, lands used by the urban poor?

We must of course recognize that project-based action alone cannot achieve changes of this kind – especially when they need far-reaching reforms. Only broader, legislative action by government can achieve that. This is the case when action is needed to increase the supply of cheap new settlement land – perhaps through new regulations allowing 'land banking' and similar operations; perhaps through changes in property taxation that force or encourage owners to bring urban land onto the market cheaply; or perhaps through laws imposing a 'ceiling' on private holdings of urban land, and releasing land holdings above this ceiling for low-income use.

But there is another kind of land market measure that can be tested and demonstrated on a project basis, that is innovations in urban land tenure. SS and SU work is well placed as a tool for innovations in this field because (as pointed out earlier in this chapter) it is one of the few kinds of action that engage the resources of different economic sectors for settlement development and housing – those of the public sector, as well as those of the private and popular sectors. All these are likely to be involved in any innovations in the field of urban land ownership and tenure, and in SS and SU projects they are already interlocked. Moreover most countries already have a body of laws and regulations that can be applied or adapted in developing alternatives to individual land ownership; for example, the various laws under which companies, co-operatives and condominiums operate. While none of this legislation may yet be directly applicable to the case, it can provide precedents adaptable to collective or co-operative land holding.

Such forms of land holding are a likely outcome of any future search for alternative urban land tenures. In this connection it is interesting to note that during the long campaign by Manila's Tondo residents for secure land title, some Tondo neighbourhoods pressed the authorities not for individual land titles but for collective title, whereby rights to the use of Tondo land and to ownership of built property would be held by members of neighbourhood associations, which would be the lessees or owners of the land itself.[3]

Political conditions in the Philippines during the 1970s perhaps made it inevitable that this option was disregarded in the actual legalizing of Tondo land occupancy. But the fact that it enjoyed local support in Tondo shows that this alternative may be practicable even in countries like the Philippines (and many others in Asia and Latin America) where the concept of individual ownership of land is deeply ingrained in both urban and rural societies.

Though we have looked here at some economic aspects of urban land holding, we cannot forget that a shared land title can have other vital dimensions for an urban community, and particularly for poor residents of a fast-growing town or city. One can foresee collective or co-operative land holding starting to provide local urban communities with a key-stone of common interests around which other forms of mutual support can find their place: for example, local enterprises backed by the equity that legal land title represents, and locally managed programmes of house-building and of social support.

In all urban societies there lies at the root of people's ambition for residential security (whether via secure land use rights, or via land ownership) the deeper drive for family security and the growing need and ambition to gain, as well as spend, some income in the housing sector. We must learn to use sites and services as one important tool in the search for ways in which fast-growing urban populations can meet their needs for both rental housing and home ownership, and for a stable community life, without merely providing further nourishment for an exploitative land and housing market.

Notes

1 The SS and SU projects in Ismailia, Egypt, provide a good example of cost recovery through differential charging for plots (see Culpin *et al.* 1978: 165–74).

2 'The improvements in the environment of slums ... have made bustees acceptable to the lower middle class. Moreover, owing to their relatively early formation, slums are excellently located in the city. As a result, both the land and the rentable value of bustees have been rapidly rising. In some areas there

has been a 100 per cent rise (from Rs 20–25 per room to Rs 40–50 per room). The natural effect of this process, however gradual, is that the poor are being forced out of the bustees on to the pavements and to the formation of new squatter settlements. And in this sense, the Bustee Improvement Programme would seem to be failing at an essential level: the protection of rights. The market process is evidently more powerful than any legal or technical process' (Roy and Sen 1980: 43ff.).

3 Professor Mary Hollnsteiner informs the writer that this was the case in the entitlement campaign of ZOTO (Zone One Tondo Organization) and of other Tondo neighbourhood associations during the early 1970s.

References

Centre for Social Research (1981) *Household Survey in Traditional Housing Areas of Lilongwe*, Lilongwe, University of Malawi.

Churchill, A. (1979) quoted in *The Urban Edge*, 3, 10.

Crooke, P. (1981) *Low Income Housing in Malawi: an Evaluation of British Aided Programmes*, London, Overseas Development Administration.

Culpin, C. *et al.* (1978) *Ismailia Demonstration Project*, London, Final Report, vol. 1.

Gondwe, E. C. R. (1981) *Future Policy on Additional Approaches in the Development of Traditional Housing Areas in Malawi*, Rotterdam, Institute for Housing Studies, Report no. 814, International Course on Housing, Planning and Building.

Malawi (1979) *Housing Situation in the Traditional Housing Estates of Blantyre and Mzuzu*, Blantyre, Malawi Housing Corporation.

Malawi (1980) *Population Census 1977, Preliminary Report*, Lilongwe, National Statistical Office.

Mangin, W. (1967) 'Latin American squatter settlements: a problem and a solution', *Latin American Research Review*, 2 (3), 65–98.

Poethig, R. P. (1971) 'The squatters of southeast Asia', *Ekistics*, 183, February, 121–5.

Roy Dilip and Jai Sen (1980) 'Calcutta's Bustee improvement programme', *Science Today*, April.

Sidhijai Tanphiphat (1980) 'Security of land tenure for slum upgrading: a case study in Bangkok', in *Human Settlements in the Development Process*, vol. 1 of the proceedings of the 7th EAROPH Congress, Kuala Lumpur, Malaysian Organization for Human Settlements, pp. 180–94.

Turner, J. F. C. (1966) 'Uncontrolled urban settlement', Working Paper 11, United Nations Interregional Seminar on Development Policies and Planning in Relation to Urbanization, Pittsburgh, United States of America.

Turner, J. F. C. (1976) *Housing by People*, London, Marion Boyars.

United Nations (1969) *Growth of the World's Urban and Rural Population 1920 to 2000*, New York, Population Studies no. 44.

United Nations (1975) 'Concept of land ownership and regional variations', in *Urban Land Policies and Land Use Control Measures*, vol. 7, Department of Economic and Social Affairs.

World Bank (1977) *Status of the Tondo Foreshore Development Project*, Washington DC.

World Bank (1978a) *Staff Appraisal Report: Philippines Tondo Foreshore Project*, Washington DC.

World Bank (1978b) *Urban Land Policy Issues and Opportunities*, Washington DC, Staff Working Paper no. 283.

World Bank (1980) *Staff Appraisal Report: Thailand National Sites and Services Project*, Washington DC.

Index